research in practice

Safeguarding in the 21st century - where to now

Jane Barlow with Jane Scott

D1428101

www.rip.org.uk

QUALITY MARK This review has been peer-reviewed by a range of service agency directors, academics, and policy practitioners committed to the development of evidence-informed practice. The authors would like to thank the following for their helpful comments: Celia Atherton, Susannah Bowyer, Sandra Campbell, Tracy Collins, Hilton Davis, Crispin Day, Stuart Gallimore, Jenny Gray, Colin Green, Anne Goldsmith, David Howe, Ruth Kingdom, Jane Lewis, Sarah Moore, Jo Tucker, and Andrew Webb.

We are grateful to the many other people who have been generous with their time and wisdom, sending us information and responding to our queries. Thanks also to staff at research in practice (and in particular Christina Walker), for their ongoing support without which this publication would not have been possible and to Steve Flood for his care and attention throughout. And finally to Val Tallis for her help with the references and her unstinting support throughout the entire process.

The views expressed in this document are those of the authors alone.

research in practice

Blacklers, Park Road

Dartington Hall, Totnes

Devon, TQ9 6EQ

e: ask@rip.org.uk

t: 01803 867692

f: 01803 868816

The full text of this review
is available on our website

www.rip.org.uk

© research in practice 2010

A CIP catalogue record is available
from the British Library

ISBN 978 1 904984 33 7 paperback

Barlow J with Scott J (2010) *Safeguarding in the 21st century –
where to now*. Dartington: research in practice

Introduction

research in practice works to make it easier for those who deliver services to children and families to access reliable research, summarised and interpreted with their particular needs in mind. This series of research reviews addresses issues identified by strategic planners, policy makers and practitioners and is of relevance whether they work in local authorities, voluntary organisations, health settings, other Children's Trust partners, central government or national organisations. The reviews are intended to shape systems, services, approaches and practice that will promote better outcomes for children and families.

This review sets out a vision of safeguarding that is fit for the twenty-first century. Its premise is that we are at a point where we need to make real changes to our approach. The last few years have seen a refocusing of safeguarding policy away from narrow interpretations of child protection to a wider vision of well-being and children's welfare needs. This shift is well supported by research, and indeed recent evidence shows falling levels of possible child abuse related deaths and greater progress in reducing such deaths in England and Wales than in most other major developed countries.

And yet there are real tensions in the system. We know that the extent of child abuse is greater than previously recognised, that there is still a real gap in its identification, and that the problems faced by the families in which it takes place are profound and multifaceted. The professions engaged in safeguarding - particularly but not only social work - highlight the problems caused by proceduralist tendencies, low tolerance of risk, low professional confidence and pressures on reflective decision-making and practice.

This review calls for a new conceptual model for safeguarding - one that will bring provision on the ground into alignment with policy and indeed go further in realising the ambition of a child-welfare approach. This means safeguarding practice that is more clearly rooted in what we know about child development. It means approaches to assessment which reflect what we know about parent-child interaction and the complexity of families' social worlds. It means an approach that sees the sustained client-practitioner relationship as key to successful therapeutic work with abusive parents and abused children. And it means organisational contexts that facilitate holistic reflective practice.

The review will be of real value to those concerned with the systems and practices used in assessment, intervention and integrated working, and to those engaged in professional training and development, across the professions engaged in safeguarding children.

Jane Lewis
Director of research in practice

contents

chapter one

The changing face of safeguarding in the 21st century

1.1 Introduction

The aim of this publication is to set out a vision of a 21st century model of safeguarding in terms of its conceptual underpinnings (Chapter Two), the assessment process (Chapter Three), the provision of targeted family support (Chapter Four), and joint working (Chapter Five). It is based on the findings from a review of both published research and a range of policy and commentary documents (see Appendix A for a description of the methods used).

Although the focus of the review is local authority children's services and social work, the findings are relevant to all practitioners whose work involves the safeguarding of children from abuse. Furthermore, it will be suggested that the model of safeguarding being proposed, particularly in terms of some of the conceptual underpinnings, are of relevance across the safeguarding spectrum, and that the care-control continuum that is continuously being negotiated by social care practitioners in particular, is better navigated using some of the approaches recommended here, many of which are typically abandoned once serious child protections concerns become an issue. Indeed, we will suggest that although there is very little 'hard' (ie randomised controlled trials) evidence about what works for 'multi-problem' and 'resistant' families, there is a broader evidence base emerging from the field of infant mental health, developmental psychology and counselling and psychotherapeutic practice more generally, which very clearly highlights the direction in which social work professionals now need to move in order to both advance the profession and to enable it to return to more effective methods of practice.

In this chapter, we start by examining some of the ongoing issues in the field of safeguarding. We then provide a brief overview of policy developments and their links with the broader social and political context. Chapter Two provides a summary of the findings about the conceptual underpinnings that the literature suggests are appropriate for a 21st century model of safeguarding, and outlines what such a model should comprise. This conceptual model is used to frame the findings throughout subsequent chapters. Chapter Three examines the evidence in relation to the assessment process; we focus in particular on evidence in relation to both the Common Assessment Framework (CAF) and the use of 'initial' and 'core' assessments undertaken by social workers. Chapter Four examines the evidence in relation to what effective working with complex families should comprise and the organisational infrastructure required to facilitate this. Chapter Five examines recent evidence in relation to integrated or joined-up working. The review covers a wide evidence base, and we have attempted to draw out the implications of the findings in Chapter Six in terms of leadership, organisational models, practice, training and workforce development.

1.2 The issues

In 2008 *The Lancet* medical journal commissioned four papers addressing what is currently *known* about child abuse. These reviews of the evidence showed that the extent of the problem was far greater than had been recognised to date, giving a prevalence in the region of 10 per cent based on data obtained from retrospective population-based surveys.[1] They highlighted important issues in terms of the identification of abuse, showing 'that few maltreated children come to the attention of child-protection agencies, indicating a failure of professionals to recognise maltreatment, failure to report, and failure of agencies to investigate or substantiate maltreatment' (Gilbert et al. 2009a). They also showed that child deaths due to maltreatment are under-recognised.

The third paper, which examined the evidence about interventions to prevent child maltreatment (ie both occurrence and recurrence) and associated impairment, showed that far more is currently known about how to prevent the primary occurrence of abuse than is known about how to prevent its recurrence (MacMillan et al. 2009).

Overall, this evidence, alongside a number of recent high-profile cases (eg Victoria Climbié and Peter Connelly), presents a rather depressing picture. The problems faced by the workforce tasked with addressing these issues were identified clearly in the Scottish Executive's report (2006) on 21st century social work:

> unreasonable expectations of what social work services can achieve

> an aversion to risk in society as a whole

> organisations restricting practice in order to protect themselves from media and political criticism

> a profession struggling with confidence levels

> decision-making ability constrained by arrangements that require escalation of decision-making up a chain of command in order to manage budgets or risk

> professional leadership eroded by pressures to manage services and budgets

> front-line workers having little idea of the values or professional priorities of their employers

> high levels of bureaucracy and inefficient systems.

Social work in Britain has been perceived to be 'in crisis' for many years but with little consensus about its nature or its remedies (Asquith, Clark, and Waterhouse 2005). A number of theorists have identified the prevailing trends towards managerialism in public services and risk-averse practice across society more generally, but there is a lack of consensus about why such changes have taken place. While some theorists, from a post-modern theoretical perspective, consider them to be a reaction to the social conditions of uncertainty and the fragmentation associated with the emergence of post-modernity and globalisation, others have explained such shifts in terms of the extensive and pervasive influence of neo-liberal political ideology (Smith and White 1997). Two themes that have been common to all explanatory models, however, are that individuals are increasingly conceptualised in modern society in ways that are 'reductionist' and that privilege rational understandings of human behaviour; and that 'there has been an increase in bureaucratic responses to the uncertainty, complexity, risk and anxiety which are inherent in social work practice' (Ruch 2005).

In response to many of these concerns, a Social Work Task Force was established in 2008. Its remit was to carry out a comprehensive review of front-line social work to identify barriers social workers face in doing their job and make recommendations for long-term reform. The final report, which was published in December 2009, identified the need for a programme of reform in addition to the Integrated Children's System already proposed (ie aimed at significantly reducing bureaucracy on the front line). It included the following key recommendations:

1. For example, a UK population-based survey of 2,869 adults aged 18 - 24 years showed that 16% reported experiencing some level of abuse, with 7% of respondents reporting serious physical abuse; 6% serious emotional abuse; 6% serious absence of care; and 1% sexual abuse involving contact (May-Chahal and Cawson 2005). Official rates indicated less than a tenth of this burden (Gilbert et al. 2009b).

> a career structure for social workers that enables experienced practitioners to progress in front-line roles as well as management (and ensures that social workers are appropriately rewarded for their work)

> a new standard to ensure that all employers put in place the conditions that social workers need to practice effectively, including high-quality supervision, time for continuing professional development, and manageable workloads

> a new and independent National College for Social Work, led and owned by the profession, to establish a stronger voice for social work and exercise appropriate influence over national policy-making and public debate; and a programme of work to improve public understanding of social work and the essential contribution social workers make

> reforms to initial social work training, so that people of high calibre enter social work and all students receive good quality education and practice-learning placements, equipping them for the challenges they will face when they begin to practice

> a new 'licensing' system that will introduce an assessed probationary year in employment for new social work graduates

> a revamped framework for continuing professional development underpinned by a practice-based masters qualification, so that all social workers can keep their skills up-to-date and develop specialist knowledge as they progress in their careers.

Chapter Two of this review examines a number of concepts that offer a view of human development and behaviour and social work practice that complement these changes and which, we will suggest, provide an appropriate conceptual basis for a 21st century model of safeguarding.

The next section of this chapter examines the policy changes that have taken place during the last ten years, and the ways in which they have altered the face of child-care practice in the UK. Although these changes have contributed to some of the problems now faced by child-care practitioners working to safeguard children, overall these policies have created a framework for safeguarding that is fit for the 21st century, and which now needs embracing and building on.

1.3 The changing face of child-care policy and practice

A wide range of political and cultural factors have shaped the ways in which public services are delivered in the UK. The landslide victory of the Labour Party in 1997 saw a continued focus on the development of performance management frameworks initiated by previous Conservative governments, across health, education and social care, with a change in the language from outputs to outcomes.

The increase in managerialism that was a significant part of the 'modernisation' agenda was underpinned by the principle that 'managers should be in control of public organisations and that they should run these organisations in line with business principles and concerns...' (Evans 2009). Two of the many consequences of this have been an increase in the proceduralism of practice, and practitioners being subject to increasing and intensive scrutiny. Recruitment difficulties within the profession, high workloads and scarce resources also contributed to the predominance of short-term methods consistent with care management (Stepney 2006).

Significant policy changes were also taking place during this period. In 1995 the government commissioned and brought together the findings from several research projects addressing issues within child protection practice - *Child Protection: Messages from research* (Department of Health 1995). It was concluded on the basis of the findings that most child protection referrals did not involve serious physical or sexual child abuse or prolonged neglect. Rather, they largely comprised children thought to be at risk of harm because of their parents' failure, for a variety of reasons (including substance misuse, inter-parental conflict, poor parenting capacities, disability, illness and poverty-induced stress), to provide protective environments. The increased focus on 'child protection', however, meant most referrals of this nature were responded to as if they were cases of serious abuse.

Research by Gibbons (1995) concluded that the child protection net was picking up too many cases inappropriately. There were concerns about the traumatic effects on children and families (Farmer and Owen 1995) and about the quality of social workers' assessments, which focused on risk rather than the needs of the child and family. In addition, section 47 investigations were contrasted less favourably with section 17 responses, where there appeared to be high levels of satisfaction among families (Tunstill and Aldgate 2000; Colton et al. 1995).

This research led to a shift in thinking at the Department of Health. All child-care referrals were to be responded to as inquiries about the needs of children, rather than as child protection investigations. Cases were to be considered as child protection when there was evidence of serious abuse or neglect that was likely to continue and to have long-term adverse consequences. More families were to be offered family support measures, particularly those who had not previously been deemed as being sufficiently high risk (ie they had not crossed the 'threshold' into child protection) (Corby 2003).

In the late 1990s, central government policy initiatives such as Quality Protects (England) and Children First (Wales) re-stated the commitment to ensuring that children were protected from emotional, physical and sexual abuse, and neglect, and set out a series of indicators by which successful intervention could be measured such as the number of child deaths, the number of re-registrations of children on child protection registers and the rate of completion of required reviews. The Quality Protects programme was launched by the Department of Health in September 1998 to support local authorities in transforming the management and delivery of children's social services. It was part of a wider set of initiatives that also included Sure Start to help children and their families get off to a better start in life, the Children's Fund to help children overcome problems as they grow up, and Connexions to support young people during their transition to adulthood and working life.

This policy shift was crystallised in a move toward focusing on children's welfare needs rather than child protection and became known as the 'refocusing initiative'. It was supported by two policy documents: *Working Together to Safeguard Children* (Department of Health, Home Office and Department for Education and Employment 1999) and the *Framework for the Assessment of Children in Need and their Families* (Department of Health 2000) a year later, which emphasised assessing children's needs first, and moving into protecting children only in serious circumstances or with the aid of further information. This policy drive gave a clear commitment to ensuring that children in need gain maximum life chances from educational opportunities, health and social care. As an important step in achieving this, it emphasised the importance of thoroughly assessing all families referred with children thought to be in need (see Chapter Three for a detailed discussion of these changes).

The publication of the Climbié Inquiry (Laming 2003) consolidated and intensified the direction of travel in the development of family policy, and pointed to the need to re-examine social care processes and to question whether changes were needed in how agencies responded to situations and families.

In 2003 the government published its green paper *Every Child Matters* (Department for Education and Skills 2003) alongside its formal response to the report into the death of Victoria Climbié (Department for Education and Skills, Department of Health and Home Office 2003). The green paper built on existing plans to strengthen preventative services by focusing on four key themes:

> increasing the focus on supporting families and carers - the most critical influence on children's lives

> ensuring necessary intervention takes place before children reach crisis point and protecting children from falling through the net

> addressing the underlying problems identified in the report into the death of Victoria Climbié - weak accountability and poor integration

> ensuring that the people working with children are valued, rewarded and trained.

Following the consultation on the green paper, the Children Act 2004 provided the legislative framework for developing more effective and accessible services focused around the needs of children, young people and families. The functions of social services previously laid out in the Children Act 1989 were unchanged, but the new act required local authorities to make arrangements to safeguard and promote the welfare of children through multiagency Children's Trusts - an integrated approach to service delivery. This followed a similar duty placed on schools by the Education Act 2002.

Revised guidance, *Working Together to Safeguard Children* (Department for Education and Skills 2006), which set out how local agencies should collaborate to keep children and young people safe, was issued to take account of these developments. A year later, the Department for Children, Schools and Families published its first *Children's Plan: Building brighter futures* (Department for Children, Schools and Families 2007a). This built on previous legislative and policy developments, informed by further consultations with professionals across agencies and by children and their families. The plan had five key principles:

> reinforcement of the message that families, not the government, bring up children

> all children have potential and should go as far as their talents can take them

> children and young people need to enjoy their childhood, as well as growing up prepared for adulthood

> services need to be shaped by and responsive to children, young people and families, and not designed around professional boundaries

> it's better to prevent failure rather than tackle a crisis.

1.4 Where are we today?

The death of Peter Connelly in 2008 resulted in extensive public vilification of the system, and social workers in particular. Some questioned whether the safeguarding initiatives had gone too far and whether social work had become too bureaucratic and insufficiently client-focused, with social workers complaining they were 'tied up in bureaucracy' (Social Work Task Force 2009).[2]

2. The debate about how social workers spend their time is a complex one. On the basis of evidence from other European countries, it has been argued that a more relevant question might in fact be whether 'given the scope (and risks and pressures) of the social work task, it is reasonable to expect social workers in England to do a job, albeit with support from less qualified workers, that is shared among members of multi-professional graduate teams in other European countries' (Boddy and Statham 2009).

However, Lord Laming's (2009) report on the progress being made nationally in the delivery of arrangements to protect children concluded that a sound legislative framework was in place and that the policy foundations were appropriate. Crucially, he stressed the importance of placing the child at the centre, and of listening to and understanding their perspective. In publishing its detailed response and action plan in May 2009, the government sought to drive forward the pace of change and called for both individual and collective action around some key principles:

> leadership and clear structures

> clear procedures

> effective information gathering and sharing

> collaboration

> flexibility (Department for Children, Schools and Families 2009).

The government accepted Lord Laming's recommendations in full and published revised guidance *Working Together to Safeguard Children: A guide to inter-agency working to safeguard and promote the welfare of children* (Department for Children, Schools and Families 2010). This sets out how organisations and individuals should now work together to safeguard and promote the welfare of children and young people in the light of Lord Laming's report and in accordance with the Children Act 1989 and the Children Act 2004.

The Social Work Task Force's final report (referred to above and published in December 2009) proposes a programme of reform that would change the face of social work. Three months after its publication, the government set out its implementation plan for taking those recommendations forward (Department for Children, Schools and Families, Department of Health and Department for Business, Innovation and Skills 2010). Furthermore, recent research comparing possible 'Child-Abuse-Related Deaths' (CARD) in England and Wales with those in other major developed countries between 1974 and 2006 found a relative 'success story', with rates of violent CARD never having been lower since records began. The findings also show that England and Wales have made significantly greater progress in reducing possible violent CARD than the majority of other major developed countries (Pritchard and Williams 2009).

1.5 Where to now?

Since the refocusing initiative began the move away from child protection toward assessment of need and safeguarding in the late 1990s and through more recent moves toward consolidation of this position, much of the concern has focused on whether children are being adequately identified and protected and what the impact of these policy changes has been in terms of families and practitioners. In order to address this, we posed a number of questions to focus our search of the evidence and broader literature.

> What should a 21st century model of safeguarding look like and what conceptual models should underpin it?

> How effective are the new models of assessment that have been introduced, and is the focus of such assessments correct?

> How should we be supporting families to change their behaviour and how do we know whether what we have done has made a difference?

> What should joined-up working look like and what is involved?

We examined the research that has been conducted during the last ten years. Based on these findings, we suggest that the model of safeguarding practice that has been heralded by recent policy changes is consistent with the innovative, advanced and holistic models of practice across Europe (particularly the Nordic countries), and that contrary to early concerns, this way of working is both effective in protecting children and more acceptable to families, particularly those for whom child protection concerns are the main reason for contact.

Furthermore, our review of the recent evidence suggests that new practices in relation to the assessment of families, involving the use of both the CAF and initial assessments, are also perceived by families more favourably and as having 'therapeutic' potential, but that these assessments are not currently being used to the widest benefit. Further effort is also needed to move more convincingly away from the assessment of 'risk' as the core method of safeguarding children, toward one of family support. We will suggest that some of the problems caused by broader managerial and proceduralist tendencies - perhaps the most important being the serious incursions that have occurred into relationship-based and reflective social work practice - need to be remedied, and that the research now points to the benefits of this type of practice.

The next chapter examines in more detail the suggested conceptual basis for a 21st century model of safeguarding, and points to a number of ways of building on the progress that has already been made using findings from the most recently published research about safeguarding practice.

chapter two

The conceptual basis for a 21st century model of safeguarding

This chapter discusses 16 concepts that can be applied at a number of levels (ie organisational, practitioner and user), and that the research suggests are fundamental to an effective 21st century model of safeguarding. Together these provide a coherent over-arching and evidence-based framework for practice.

2.1 Introduction

Policy changes over the past decade (see Chapter One) have created the context for a model of safeguarding that has at its heart the promotion of the well-being of all children, and indeed, recognition of children's right not only to protection but to optimal conditions in which to grow and develop (Committee on the Rights of the Child 1989). These policy developments are consistent with recent evidence, which strongly suggests the need to move in the direction of a child and family welfare model of safeguarding. Recent research also points, however, to the need for child-care practitioners generally, and social workers more specifically, to develop a more holistic understanding of individual functioning - one that embraces the 'complexity, ambiguity and uncertainty that characterises human behaviour and people's lives' and thereby the professional worker-client relationship (Ruch 2005). This research suggests that the orthodox, technical-rational understandings of knowledge that have emerged alongside some of the policy changes, and which have been described as 'desperate attempts to cling on to certainty and eliminate risk through the application of increasingly proceduralised responses to the challenges of practices...', now need changing because they have proved fruitless (Ruch 2005).

This chapter will bring together a number of concepts which the research suggests are fundamental to effective safeguarding, and which will be used to define the approach adopted throughout the remainder of this publication. The concepts that have been selected for inclusion have all been the subject of considerable research and debate over the past ten years and can be applied at a number of levels - systems-level, practice-level, and user-level. These categories, however, are not exclusive, and concepts that have, for the purpose of our discussion, been organised as user-level could equally be defined as system-level concepts within another context. Neither is this list definitive. It seems likely there are other concepts that could complement the list assembled here and that it should be extended as time progresses.

2.2 Underpinning concepts

Overview

Box 2.1 summarises the core concepts that our review of the evidence has highlighted as being fundamental to a 21st century model of safeguarding. They are consistent with recent policy developments such as *Think Family: Improving the life chances of families at risk* (Cabinet Office 2007), and the application of these concepts across the safeguarding continuum would address some of the practice issues that have emerged during the past two decades. They provide the basis for an advanced model of practice that should be embraced both by managers and practitioners working across children's services.

Although individually these concepts address very different issues, jointly they represent a coherent and comprehensive underpinning model for safeguarding, and the most appropriate basis for practice at this stage of our knowledge development.

Box 2.1: Conceptual underpinnings for a 21st century model of safeguarding

From...	To...
Organisational level	
Service-based	Outcomes-based
Child protection focus	Child and family welfare approach
Tradition-based	Multidimensionally evidence-based
Multidisciplinary	Transdisciplinary
Systems	Complexity
Social constructionism	Critical realism
Practitioner level	
Systemic	Relational
Solution-focused	Relationship-based
Expert	Partnership-based
Rule-based/procedural	Reflective
Child-centred	Family-centred
Child or parent-focused	Dyadic
Deficit-based	Resilience/strengths-based
User level	
Isolationist	Transactional-ecological
Cognitive development	Social and emotional development
Authoritarian	Participatory

Although it is not possible to do full justice to many of these concepts in the context of this publication,[1] the following sections of this chapter provide an overview of each of them in terms of the underpinning evidence and their relevance to the issue of safeguarding. We conclude by proposing a framework which demonstrates the way in which they are linked within an overarching model of practice (see Figure 2.3).

1. It is recommended that the reader consult some of the referenced texts for a fuller exposition.

Organisational level

Outcomes-based

During the past ten years there has been a gradual shift away from service-focused approaches to what has been termed an 'outcomes focused' approach. The aim of this move has been to encourage children's services practitioners to structure their activities not in terms of inputs or processes, but by focusing on the difference that their activities should make in terms of the outcomes for children. *Every Child Matters: Change for children* (Department for Education and Skills 2004) placed such outcomes-based approaches at the heart of service delivery. Some of the key features of an outcomes-based approach are highlighted in Box 2.2.

> ### Box 2.2: Key features of an outcomes-based approach
>
> > **Outcomes-based accountability.** This involves a much clearer understanding of what overall outcomes are sought for children, and what quantifiable improvements in their welfare and well-being would be required to achieve them (current measures are too often about process and delivery targets, rather than results).
>
> > **Community collaboration.** This is based on the idea that no single organisation, service or individual should be expected to shoulder the responsibility for improving the well-being of children and families. Accountability for achieving results should be a shared and collaborative responsibility within a community.
>
> > **Participation by individual citizens, families and children.** This requires genuine participation, which is rarely to be found in examples of what are currently portrayed as 'public consultation'.
>
> > **Innovative financial strategies.** Traditional financial systems often inhibit both community involvement and much-needed service improvements. Agencies need to pool resources and to use funds more flexibly to recognise local priorities. (Utting, Rose and Pugh 2001 cited in McAuley and Cleaver 2006)

One study that examined the extent to which five organisations in England had adopted an outcomes-based approach and the difference it had made, found that although the organisations were at different levels of change, all five had developed 'new partnerships within and across agencies.' They each had 'a new focus and an overall more unified approach to their work', and an 'increasingly developed view of the importance of using measures which capture change in moving towards improved outcomes' (McAuley and Cleaver 2006).

An outcomes-based approach is the starting point for our conceptual framework and the five Every Child Matters outcomes (of which 'staying safe' is one) are the specific outcomes to which practitioners are viewed as working.

Child and family welfare approach

Over the last ten years, policies governing the response to maltreatment in the UK have moved from a 'child protection' model, towards a 'child and family welfare' approach to safeguarding. This involves a focus on the identification of children in need and the provision of much earlier support and services, in contrast to the earlier emphasis on the identification and investigation of maltreatment, and the assessment of future risk.

Research that examined the differences between these two approaches across 12 European countries found better outcomes, particularly in terms of integration, in those countries implementing child and family-welfare focused systems (Katz and Hetherington 2006). Recent research suggests that the best outcomes for children may in fact be the product of systems that manage to balance the best elements of both service types of approach (Gilbert et al. 2009a).

The child and family welfare conceptual model has major implications in terms of both assessing families (with the emphasis now being on 'need' as opposed to 'risk' *per se*) and the provision of appropriate services (see for example, *Think Family: Improving the life chances of families at risk* - Cabinet Office 2007). These issues will be examined in more depth in Chapter Three, which focuses on assessment, and Chapter Four, which focuses on intervention. Perhaps most importantly in terms of assessment, we will suggest that the findings now point very strongly to the value of what has been defined as 'a third generation' approach, which consists of 'empirically validated, structured decision-making' (White and Walsh 2006) or 'structured clinical judgement'.
This involves the use of clinical expertise both to undertake contextual assessments and to make decisions about the necessary standardised tools to be used as part of an actuarial assessment of risk. Clinical judgement/skills are then used to translate the information from both of these processes into decision-making about evidence-based interventions and services, alongside the application of information drawn from a range of other sources, including client preferences and choices, cultural factors etc.

Figure 2.1: Cycle of evidence-based practice. Model adapted from Haynes, Devereaux and Guyatt (2002) as presented in Shlonsky and Wagner (2005)

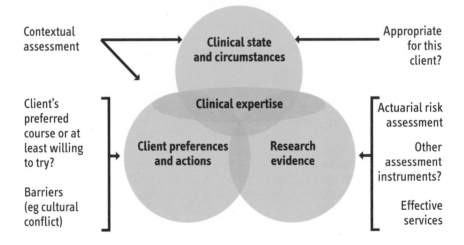

In terms of service provision, this approach points very clearly to the importance of intervening early to provide families with evidence-based support with the aim of preventing abuse by promoting children's well-being and supporting families. The Family Nurse Partnership (Rowe 2009) provides a prime example of this type of intervention. The evidence now also supports the use of relationship-based working and this is one of the practitioner-level concepts that are discussed below.

Perhaps most importantly, this approach is consistent with the implementation of multidimensional evidence-based practice that is examined in the next section.

Multidimensional evidence-based practice

Evidence-based[2] practice has now been broadly adopted in the UK and underpins most health and, increasingly, social care policy. An evidence-based approach is an improvement on authority-based practice in that it involves greater transparency, accountability, attention to ethical issues, and service-user and provider perspectives, even though there is little evidence currently regarding the extent to which these are actually implemented at the level of front-line practice (Gray, Plath and Webb 2009). Evidence-based practice involves addressing the extent to which knowledge from research can be applied locally, in conjunction with ethical issues such as informed consent, client values and expectations (Petr 2009). For example, it is suggested that there are four cornerstones of evidence-based practice in social work:

> what we know from research and theory

> professional wisdom and values

> what we have learned from personal experience, and

> what clients bring to practice situations.

And further, that 'social workers should not blindly apply or impose research findings to every individual client, but instead use their own experience as well as the client's preferences to honor client self-determination' (Petr 2009).

Petr distinguishes between evidence-based practice as a process (or verb), and as a validated intervention (or noun). The former refers to the process of posing a question, identifying evidence with which to answer it, critically appraising the evidence, and applying the results to practice and policy, and as such takes into account consumer and professional perspectives. Evidence-based practice as a noun refers to the application of programmes and interventions that have been empirically validated.

'Best practices' are defined as 'those treatments or interventions that have been shown to be effective through rigorous scientific research' (Petr 2009). Petr has rightly suggested, however, that 'what works' should not be defined narrowly as 'quantitative evidence' but should include data from a range of sources. Such an approach does not limit knowledge to information that has been obtained using a positivist paradigm, and is more broadly consistent with the critical realist approach (discussed below), which highlights the need to move away from an assessment of 'what works' using randomised controlled trials, to assessing what works, for whom, in what circumstances (eg Pawson and Tilley 1997), utilising mixed research methods (ie the iterative use of both quantitative and qualitative data). Indeed, mixed methods are becoming more widely accepted within post-positivist paradigms more generally, and organisations such as the Cochrane Collaboration and large funding councils such as the Medical Research Council now encourage the combined use of both types of data.

2. Evidence-based practice may also be referred to as evidence-informed practice, but for consistency, we have used the former term within this review.

Petr suggests, however, that what is still missing from this model is 'a value-critical analysis that juxtaposes the best practice findings against the preferred values and principles that guide service delivery', including those of adequacy, equity and efficiency. He suggests that multidimensional evidence-based practice involves not only assessing what best practices are, but what they could be, and that this involves relevant best practices being measured and judged against evaluative criteria that are aimed at improving practices and outcomes for clients. This involves the following seven steps:

1. identify the multidimensional evidence-based practice question

2-4. identify multiples sources of knowledge and evidence pertaining to the multidimensional evidence-based practice question using the following sources - consumers, professionals and research (both quantitative and qualitative)

5. summarise findings of best practices across all three perspectives

6-7. critique current best practice in terms of its 'potency' and the application of 'value criteria' (Petr 2009).

We will suggest throughout this publication that many of the 'interventions' and 'programmes' that are used in the field of safeguarding typically comprise a relationship between two people. This is particularly true of social work, for example, where although the relationship is not an end in itself, it is nevertheless a core part of the process or mechanism through which change is achieved (see Chapter Four). The worker-client relationship is therefore an intervention in the sense that it is being used to facilitate change in the family. This means that as with other so-called interventions, we need to make certain that such relationship working is underpinned by evidence in terms of ensuring that it is likely to bring about the desired change. In order to do this we need to be clear about: a) what factors we are trying to change; and b) which aspects of the relationship (intervention) will affect such change. This requires that:

> interventions are explicitly based on a theoretical model of change, optimally in the form of a logic model that targets the relevant epidemiological factors

> intervention goals are clearly articulated as part of the logic model

> intervention activities are designed to produce outcomes that will achieve those goals

> the logic model should also specify the target group or audience for which an intervention is intended and the level for which change is targeted (eg individual, family, school or community) (Petr 2009).

There are now a number of resources to help practitioners to achieve this (eg Programme Planning Evaluation Toolkit, University of Wisconsin Extension, described in Petr 2009).

The application of evidence to practice is at the heart of this publication, and will inform the recommendations made throughout the remaining chapters.

Transdisciplinary working

Greater collaboration between health, education and social services has been identified by a number of key government documents such as *Every Child Matters* (Department for Education and Skills 2003) in order to meet the needs of children more effectively. This includes the use of 'flexibilities' such as pooled budgets, lead commissioning, integrated provision and key workers (Sloper 2004).

A number of concepts have been used to describe collaboration between agencies, including multi or interagency, multi/interdisciplinary, joint/team working and partnerships, and a number of recent systematic reviews have examined the evidence in relation to integrated or joined-up working in terms of practices across a wide range of services in both the UK (Worrall-Davies and Cottrell 2009; Lord et al. 2008; Robinson, Atkinson and Downing 2008a, 2008b; Anning et al. 2006; Sloper 2004) and Europe (Katz and Hetherington 2006). Although much of the literature has attempted to identify the best model of integrated working, recent research has begun to 'move away from the view of integrated services as the ideal model, towards a view that the outcomes of integrated working are situation specific and that diverse approaches to the degree or extent may be equally valid' (Robinson, Atkinson and Downing 2008a, 2008b).

Sloper (2004) uses the term 'transdisciplinary' to classify multiagency services based on 'the ways in which the professionals work together at an operational level, alongside the extent of holistic and partnership working with families'. She suggests that 'multidisciplinary working' refers to practice among individuals working within a single agency where the focus tends to be on the priorities of that agency and co-ordination with other agencies is rare. 'Interdisciplinary working' refers to a situation in which individual professionals from different agencies separately assess the needs of child and family, and then meet together to discuss findings and set goals. The only truly holistic model centred on the needs of the child and family is 'transdisciplinary working'. This refers to a model of working in which members of different agencies work together jointly, sharing aims, information, tasks and responsibilities.

> *[This] involves a primary provider, whose post is funded on a multiagency basis, playing a key role in designing and delivering a programme of care, and co-ordinating services. This person acts as a key worker and takes responsibility for delivery of a unified programme of care for the child and family. One co-ordinated multiagency assessment is undertaken and used by all professionals. Families are seen as equal partners.* (Sloper 2004)

This model of transdisciplinarity is consistent with a model of the hybrid professional who works within a range of multidisciplinary settings, but also recognises the value of different professional skills and identities. Chapter Five will examine recent evidence about the ways in which such transdisciplinary working can be achieved, alongside a number of innovative models of safeguarding practice that are now being applied (eg Reclaiming Social Work in Hackney).

Complexity

The customer-citizenship model that is at the heart of the modernisation process to which children's services have been subjected over the past 20 years is underpinned by principles of efficiency, predictability, calculability and control (Harris 2009). Furthermore, such principles are underpinned by a linear view of processes and a rational model of man, and have led to the policy premise and public conviction that 'we can develop systems that can ensure that no child will die' (Lonne et al. 2008). However, recent theorising that has applied complexity theory to child welfare (Rowlands 2009) and safeguarding (Payne 2008; Stevens and Cox 2008; Stevens and Hassett 2007) suggests that the continued pursuit of systems that are aimed at minimising risk irrespective of the other costs, such as the associated loss of reflective practice, gives rise to a blame culture when a child is harmed, which further undermines the functioning of the organisation (see below for further discussion).

Complexity theory questions the appropriateness of such systems and offers an alternative framework for conceptualising safeguarding practice (eg Payne 2008; Stevens and Cox 2008). Much safeguarding practice (eg Department of Health 2000) is currently underpinned by a traditional systems model (Stevens and Cox 2008), which focuses on strengths as well as difficulties, and identifies tasks that families have to perform in order to function along a number of dimensions (eg organisation and character). For Stevens and Cox the problem with the systems theory approach is that it suggests that 'by knowing about the component parts of the system, and by analysing how these interact with each other, an intervention can be applied in one part of the system which will have a predictable effect on another part of the system'. Stevens and Cox (2008) contrast this position with complexity theory, which recognises that families are 'complex adaptive systems' and that the factors that lead to a child being harmed within a family have the ability to undergo spontaneous self-organisation (see Box 2.3), and that these become more complex with the addition of systems to protect the child or intervene with the family.

> Box 2.3: Self-organising systems
>
> 'A complex adaptive system has a pattern and, from this pattern, a range of likely outcomes can be indicated, but not predicted. Indeed, some of the outcomes will be unforeseen. Given the dynamic and live nature of the complex adaptive system, linear analysis of risk is inappropriate. Non-linear approaches to working with risk are much more relevant to the real nature of the system surrounding the child.' (Stevens and Cox 2008)

Stevens and Cox use the example of a weather system to demonstrate the way in which principles derived from complexity theory have relevance to safeguarding. Weather arises due to an interaction of factors and this combination creates a complex adaptive system able to undergo self-organisation. This means that while we can know that a particular set of factors is likely to lead to a hurricane, it is nevertheless not possible to predict when or whether such hurricanes will occur. The factors that lead to children being harmed can similarly be viewed in this way: practitioners can identify factors that contribute to the occurrence of abuse, but have difficulty predicting whether or when harm will occur.

This method of conceptualising safeguarding work has implications in terms of assessment, for example, because viewing families as complex systems in this way, raises questions regarding the appropriateness of applying 'predictive' models of risk assessment, and points instead towards the need for 'indicative', non-linear methods of assessing risk (see Box 2.4).

> Box 2.4: Non-linear approaches to risk assessment
>
> Complexity theory advocates a non-linear approach. For example, it is suggested that:
>
> 'a practitioner trying to operate a system of risk assessment in child protection from a stance of adding up the risk factors is applying linear understanding. In linear understanding, A plus B always equals C. Complexity theory suggests that this is not an adequate way to deal with complex phenomena, such as assessing the risk of harm to a child. This is because the development of complex adaptive systems is not a linear process. It is non-linear. In other words, action A plus B may lead to action C, but it may also lead to actions D, E and/or F. On the other hand, it may lead to no change. Coveney and Highfield (1996) suggest that complexity theory allows the development of indicative models, not predictive models of risk.' (Stevens and Cox 2008)

The development of indicative (rather than predictive) methods of assessment is consistent with the wider evidence about the low accuracy of tools that are aimed at predicting whether abuse will occur (see for example, Peters and Barlow 2003), and the suggested need to develop integrated approaches to assessment (see Chapter Three). Complexity theory thus suggests that while operational standards and procedures enable practitioners to make sense of what is happening in a complex situation, simply following current procedures does not automatically mean a child is safe from harm, and that increasing the number of procedures will not improve the 'accuracy' of the assessment process. Further, it is suggested that 'non-linear understanding insists upon close attention to the impact that the smallest details can have upon the whole system for it is sometimes the smallest changes that can have the biggest effect' (Stevens and Cox 2008).

Complexity theory also suggests that a linear approach to risk actually gives rise to a blame culture if a child is harmed, and that exposure to criticism of this nature acts as an attractor that pushes the organisational system to the edge of chaos or towards a 'dissipative structure'. The impact on the roles of practitioners is to tip the balance of work towards child protection and away from care and support (Stevens and Cox 2008).

A number of other aspects of complexity theory are relevant to helping us understand safeguarding more accurately. Lewin (1999) argues that group behaviour on a small scale reflects the milieu within which it is embedded. Thus, behaviour within families may appear chaotic, but may actually be responding to the laws of complexity, one of which is 'emergence'. Emergence refers to the way in which the sum can be more than the individual parts, or in terms of safeguarding, the way in which a set of factors can give rise to a particular outcome such as abuse, but in a way that could not have been predicted by or indeed reduced to the individual component parts. This phenomenon can be seen to operate at the level of teams. For example, social welfare teams may have the same number of staff representing the same professions with the same number of children and cover similar areas of population, but act, feel and respond very differently (Stevens and Cox 2008). In terms of safeguarding, this model suggests that emergence needs to be 'facilitated' rather than 'controlled' to create safe conditions for children.

Overall, in terms of safeguarding, complexity theory suggests children are part of complex systems that are neither completely deterministic nor completely random. The implication of this is the need for organisational structures that enable practitioners to work within such boundaries of instability, and that encourage ways of working that recognise that structural measures may not suffice to protect children. Instead organisations need to:

> develop a sense of dynamism within the system and view all factors as potential contributors to abrupt shift or change

> have a high degree of tolerance to working within boundaries of instability or intolerance

> develop the confidence to move away from a risk-averse linear approach and towards complex adaptive theory because what we find when we search is a function of how we look (Lissack 1996).

Complexity theory thus provides professionals working within the field of safeguarding with a better framework for practice. Other recent work on complexity in relation to children in need has similarly concluded that 'linear thinking' in children's welfare is misconceived because such issues 'are too complex to be susceptible to linear, reductionist thinking' and that 'the government is right to shift the focus away from social services centrality and instead try to knit all child and family agencies together to achieve a concerted response' (Rowlands 2009).

Critical realism

The case-work tradition within social work that focuses attention at the level of individuals in terms of the importance of hearing the life story and narratives of service users, alongside the desire for participative practice among child-care workers more generally, has contributed to the view that such practice should be underpinned by a 'social constructionist' view of the world. Social constructionism suggests that social interactions are the basis of all knowledge, and that all social phenomena are socially constructed. Attempts to know the 'real' or 'objective' world[3] are hampered by the fact we are all socially and culturally situated, and by the fact that we need to use language to access and describe it.

While this stance in and of itself is not being called into question, the philosophical principles underpinning social constructionism are problematic, particularly for practitioners working in the field of safeguarding. First, this approach prevents us from thinking and theorising about the way in which the 'real objective world' impacts on the lives of clients. This results in practice that is overly individualistic and that fails to take account of constraints imposed by social structures.

A second but related point is that social constructionism maintains that all attempts to know the real world are prevented by the social and cultural location of individuals. This leads to the kind of relativism that sits somewhat uncomfortably with the need a) to prioritise basic rights (ie the child's right to live without fear of his/her caretakers) over cultural practices (ie cultural endorsement of parenting practices such as physical punishment); and b) to be able to prioritise some accounts of events over others. Safeguarding practice is premised on the assumption that some aspects of a child's environment may be 'objectively harmful' to the child.

These problems are addressed by critical realism, which both provides a 'theory of human agency whilst at the same time taking account of the impact of the social structure' (Houston 2001). This provides a model of the way in which the world is socially constructed, which recognises the significance not only of the individual and their narrative but of an objective world that exists independently of our ability to know about it and that constrains the activities of individuals. It has therefore been suggested that critical realism is a more appropriate model for safeguarding and social workers in particular, because it both provides a theory of human agency while addressing the structures that determine, constrain and oppress our activities in a way that social constructionism precludes. By 'offering an explanation of the structural impediments to human development it facilitates programmes that lead to the emancipatory transformation of those structures' (Houston 2001).

Practitioner level

Relational

Systemic theory has over the years become core to the working of many practitioners within the field of safeguarding, and in particular social work. It has been suggested that this is because it offers a specialist practice knowledge to social workers that is consistent with the broader philosophy underpinning social work (Flaskas 2007). Systemic ideas originated in the physical sciences in the 1940s and are the basis of family therapy, which Flaskas suggests 'emerged as a struggle to broaden the intensely individualistic focus of the psychotherapeutic services of the time'. Since then, systemic practices have evolved to include 'the exploration of the multiple contexts affecting

3. More radical versions of this strand of idealism and individualism would suggest that nothing exists beyond ideas or individuals, ie there is no 'objective' world.

family life' including the importance of social and political contexts (eg gender, race, culture, class and sexuality) and such practices need to be retained.

Over the past decade, however, a number of ideas and concepts from the field of attachment and psychoanalytic theory have begun to intersect with this broader systemic framework (Flaskas 2007). Psychoanalytic practice has become increasingly 'relational' during this time, and research about 'attachment' has provided a significant empirical basis for this alongside a recognition of the importance of the client's lived experiences. This relational trend, which will be examined in more detail in the next section (see also Chapter Four), has been underpinned by an increase in knowledge concerning the development of the self within the context of relationships. For example, research from the field of developmental psychology shows that early relationship patterns are developed in interaction with primary caregivers and internalised in the form of 'internal working models' that are stored as procedural memories. These are not therefore under conscious control and strongly influence later relationship patterns (Schore 1994). This is consistent with the psychoanalytic emphasis on the importance of the unconscious mind, including the recognition that human behaviour can be significantly influenced by such unconscious thoughts.

The psychoanalytic concept of 'transference' refers to the way in which such early relationship patterns are re-enacted within later relationships (including relationships with partners, children and in the context of a client-worker relationship); 'counter-transference' refers to the complex interaction of the worker's 'unconscious processes and the clients' ways of relating' (Schore 1994). These ideas will be explored more fully in Chapter Four, where it will be suggested that such concepts are important to effective relationship-based practice, particularly with families in which there are safeguarding concerns.

Similarly, empirical research from infant mental health that has focused on patterns of caregiver-infant interaction has played a significant role in informing the 'relational turn' in psychotherapeutic theory and practice. Alongside concepts from attachment and neuroscience, this research has significantly improved our understanding of both the aetiology of child abuse and also the importance of 'relationship-based' practice. For example, empirical research has identified the importance of what has been termed 'proto-conversational turn-taking', which occurs between the primary carer and infant. This refers to repeated patterns of interaction that are characterised by 'attunement (the co-ordination of affective states), rupture (the lapse of mutual co-ordination) and repair (the re-establishment of co-ordination under new conditions)' (Walker 2008). This sequence of attunement, rupture and repair, which is described in Box 2.5, is repeated continuously as part of the ongoing interaction between parent and infant, and forms the basis of later internal working models.[4] These interactions are important because they help the infant to regulate his or her emotions.

However, where the infant's emotional states trigger profound discomfort in the parent (eg where there is unresolved loss or trauma, mental health problems or drug/alcohol abuse, or where there is domestic violence etc), interaction may become characterised by withdrawal, distancing or neglect (ie omission) or intrusion in the form of blaming, shaming, punishing and attacking (ie commission) (Walker 2008). Repeated experiences of this nature lead to deep-seated feelings of anger and shame that disrupt the infant's development, and which are then repeated in later relationships.

---

4. Stern (1998) referred to these as Representations of Interactions that are Generalisable (RIGs).

> **Box 2.5: Attunement, rupture and repair in a mother and infant**
>
> 'Attuned mutual co-ordination between mother and infant occurs when the infant's squeal of delight is matched by the mother's excited clapping and sparkling eyes. The baby then becomes over-stimulated, arches its back and looks away from the mother. A disruption has occurred and there is a mis-coordination: the mother, still excited, is leaning forward, while the baby, now serious, pulls away. However, the mother then picks up the cue and begins the repair: she stops laughing and, with a little sigh, quietens down. The baby comes back and makes eye contact again. Mother and baby gently smile. They are back in sync again, in attunement with each other.' (Walker 2008)

This evidence is not only important in terms of our understanding of the developmental needs of young children and about what constitutes adverse early parenting (Barlow and Schrader McMillan 2010), but as will be argued in Chapter Four, it is also key to the success of therapeutic work with parents who abuse their children, many of whom will have experienced early care-giving that was characterised by a lack of attunement or an absence of repair to ruptures. These concepts help us to understand why such parents experience intense feelings of anger, fear and shame when disruption occurs in relationships in adult life, and why they are also highly vulnerable to feeling misunderstood and not listened to (see Box 2.6 and Walker 2008). It will also be suggested in Chapter Four that not only is an understanding of such processes key to effective working with 'multi-problem' families, but it is also key to the functioning of child welfare organisations (Mandin 2007) and, in particular, to effective communication between professionals. It is suggested, for example, that rupture followed by a lack of repair characterised much of the miscommunication referred to in the Climbié Inquiry (Walker 2008).

> **Box 2.6: A relational approach and organisational functioning**
>
> '[Concepts that] have been developed to make sense of the inner world of infants, and the ways in which such early development can be seriously derailed by non-optimal parenting, can also be applied in terms of the wider professional system and organisations.' (Mandin 2007)

Relationship-based working

It has been suggested that recruitment difficulties within the profession, high workloads and scarce resources have resulted in a predominance of short-term methods in safeguarding that are consistent with care management (Stepney 2006). The use of such methods has been further increased by the frequency and critical outcome of inquiries into child deaths, and by an increasing anxiety among practitioners, and a prevailing culture of blame.

The importance of building a trusting relationship with clients has been acknowledged and emphasised by a range of helping professions, including social work, psychotherapy, nursing and medicine. However, there has been wide variation within these professions in the extent to which the relationship itself has been regarded as being a central part of professional practice. Recent findings in relation to safeguarding suggest this is one area in which the relationship between client and practitioner is core to effective working. For example, a recent overview of the evidence about effective interventions for complex families where there were concerns about (or evidence of) a child suffering significant harm, showed the importance of providing a 'dependable professional relationship' for parents and children, in particular with those families who conceal or minimise their difficulties (Thoburn 2009). Thoburn suggests that such cases are likely to require a long-term relationship with children's social services, and that 'continuity of support is essential for complex families with whom change is hard to achieve or maintain'.

The importance of relationship-based working has recently been demonstrated by two studies that focused on social work. Knei-Paz (2009) found it was the quality of the therapeutic bond established between social worker and client that was the basis for what was conceived of as a positive intervention. The bond 'acquired significance and was perceived as successful to the extent that it assumed personal rather than bureaucratic dimensions'. The study found that as a result of this bond, clients often experienced a 'significant relief from the weight of their distress and reported changes in self-image and in their family relations'. However, the study also found that heavy workloads, extensive bureaucracy and budgetary limitations made it difficult to focus on developing this bond.

Another recent qualitative study of client experiences of receiving care from their social workers also indicated the need for potentially radical shifts in how the worker-client relationship is conceptualised within social work practice (Alexander and Charles 2009). This study found that although social workers described their ability to attend to, create and manage variability in the levels of intimacy within each relationship and between clients, mutuality was viewed by participants as subversive, reflecting a disconnection between social work training and practice in the field.

There has been a strong tradition in some professions, including social work, of psychodynamically informed practice, which focuses on the relationship established between professional and client, and which recognises that it is 'within the relationship that most of the important things happen, for good or ill' (Howe 1998). Views about relationship-based practice within social work have been equivocal, however (Ruch 2005), and its use at different points in time has tended to reflect dominant socio-political ideology. It has been suggested, though, that the recent explosion of empirical enquiry and theory development has increased 'confidence in the centrality of the relationship in human behaviour and development' (Howe 1998),[5] and the body of research that has emerged over the last decade in the field of infant mental health, developmental psychology and neuroscience has further confirmed this stance. This evidence will be examined in further detail in Chapter Four, where it will be suggested that the client-worker relationship is a central part of the process of bringing about change when it is underpinned by some of the concepts examined here because it can:

> function as an emotionally restorative experience

> meet some of the unmet dependency needs of clients, thereby helping them to function better in their parental role

> help clients to develop understanding about the impact of their own life experiences on their parenting, and

> serve as a model for other relationships.

Some of the core skills involved in relationship-based practice (eg relational awareness, authenticity, openness, mutual respect, responsiveness and presence - Freedberg 2008) are also core to partnership working, which we will suggest is a central aspect of relationship-based practice and is examined in the next section.

---

5. Howe goes on to cite evidence from three areas: i) counselling and psychotherapy, which have focused on the qualities of the helping relationship and the therapeutic alliance; ii) social and interpersonal psychology, which has focused on the characteristics of adult relationships; and iii) developmental psychology, which has focused on the importance of close relationships in the formation of personality (see also Howe submitted and Howe 2005).

Partnership working

Partnership working with families has been defined in *Every Child Matters* as involving: the active involvement both of parents and practitioners; equality with regard to decision-making; complementary expertise (ie that in which parents are recognised to have skills and knowledge in relation to their own child); negotiation and agreement of aims and processes; mutuality; and respect.

Effective partnership is based on agreement of aims, of goals, and of the means to achieving those goals. However, it's unrealistic to expect everyone to agree on everything, so a partnership relationship must be founded on respectful negotiation. (Negotiation and agreement could be supported and outcomes recorded using the *Early Support Family Service Plan*.)

A recent study found that what parents wanted from formal support services that are provided in the context of identified child abuse was a move from 'unequal and adversarial relationships to ones that are more collaborative and co-operative' (see Box 2.7).

Box 2.7: Response to partnership working

'I've got to admit, most child protection officers and offices are pretty nasty, but I found that the one in [name] here, they're actually quite nice... They're just more [pauses to think] they listen more - and they actually take in what you're saying and don't say "Oh yeah, we don't like the way you're doing this, this is how you should be doing it blah blah blah"... They [name] listen to what we have to say and...they told us how they wanted things to go and actually asked us how we wanted things to go instead of telling us, "Okay, this has to happen and this has to happen and this has to happen", but yeah, they let us ... make some of the decisions as well, which is good. It's one less stress.'
Susan quoted in Hardy and Darlington (2008)

In recent years the term 'partnership' has been conflated in policy documents so that it incorporates partnership working between agencies, as well as partnership working with families (Bain 2009). But 'working in partnership' with families was one of the key premises underpinning *Working Together to Safeguard Children* (Department of Health, Home Office and Department of Education and Employment 1999), which set out 15 'basic principles' for such work. It has been suggested, however, that these 15 underlying 'partnership' principles can actually be divided into two groups, with the first aimed at safeguarding social workers against accusations of professional misconduct and minimising complaints, and the second emphasising 'the need for the careful exercise of statutory powers in the context of child protection' (Bain 2009). It is further suggested that only one of the 15 principles demonstrates any sort of understanding of partnership working that has anything in common with broader understandings of such practice in terms of it being 'a contractual agreement among equals' (Bain 2009).

Indeed, Bain suggests that 'the concept of partnership adopted in these policy documents tends to confirm and reinforce the existing power relationship between social workers and parents', and queries whether the power relationship between social workers and parents actually 'prevents the possibility of a partnership based on an agreement among equals' (ie on the grounds that social workers ultimately have the power to remove a child from the parent). Thoburn (2009) similarly raises the question as to whether it is possible to work collaboratively with parents or whether an element of coercion is needed (ie through the formal child protection procedures or the family justice or criminal courts). She shows that the 'partnership-compulsion' continuum has been the subject of a number of studies (Thoburn 2009), and suggests that government statistics demonstrate major differences between similar authorities in the rate at which children's names are placed on the child protection register or are subject to a formal child protection plan (ie use of compulsion), and that the differences across national boundaries are just as great (Thoburn 2009).[6]

It will be suggested in Chapters Three and Four that the research shows that the process of working in partnership provides practitioners with the skills to establish a contractual process of working that is mutual, open, honest, respectful and empathic (Thoburn 2009), and that enables practitioners to stand alongside parents as supporters and advocates. Moreover, and contrary to current practice, it will be suggested that such partnership working should be at the heart of practice where there are serious concerns about the safety of the child. We will also summarise evidence to show that evidence-based partnership methods of working of this nature are also essentially goal-focused and change-oriented (Davis and Day 2010; Harnett and Day 2008; Keatinge, Fowler and Briggs 2008), and that a fundamental part of the process of working in partnership to bring about change is the development of reflective and critical practitioners at an organisational level.

Reflective, critical practitioners

Both recent research (see Burton 2009) and enquiry reports (see Laming 2003; 2009) have pointed to the need to improve the capacity of professionals to think critically about the families and children with whom they work, for children's services to develop 'a dialectic or reflective mindset', and for managers to create a 'learning culture' (Burton 2009).

One of the difficulties in defining reflective practice is a result of its dual function, in which 'it both generates knowledge through the reflective process and is the vehicle by which it is applied to practice' (Burton 2009).

Crawshaw (2008) observes that the achievement and maintenance of professional competence requires social workers to be reflective and that this involves:

> being critically aware of what we are being asked to do (by our agency and by government policy)

> being critically aware of the social context within which people live their lives - and how lives are constrained or encouraged by that context

> being curious and analytical about the behaviours and actions of the people to whom we are providing a service

> being analytical and ethical about the ways in which we provide services or interventions in order to ensure they are of maximum effectiveness (using ethical measures).

---

6. Thoburn (2009) points to the need for authorities to use the technique of 'survival analysis' to assist in understanding how such formal processes are used.

Recent research that examined practitioner understandings of reflective practice and its operationalisation (Ruch 2005) found that 'holistically reflective' practitioners adopted more 'relationship-based' and 'risk-taking' approaches to their practice, in contrast with 'technically reflective' practitioners, who were more inclined to focus on 'what they did and how, with a view to doing it better next time'. The latter group was less inclined to ask 'why' questions and more inclined to 'exhibit more restrictive and prescriptive responses to practice situations, and find it more difficult to establish responsive, relationship-based approaches'.

Ruch (2005) suggests, however, that one of the key obstacles to both relationship-based and reflective practice is the continued application of reductionist models of human behaviour, which conceptualise individuals in purely rational terms. She suggests there is a need to re-conceptualise both the client and the practitioner in social work practice, such that his or her emotional responses and the emotional impact of practice on him or her are acknowledged.

While social workers in the 1950s and 60s were cautioned to maintain firm boundaries - on the grounds that such 'transference' and 'counter-transference' reactions could distort the relationship (Freedberg 2008) - learning since then (mostly from psychotherapeutic research) has enabled a range of practitioners to begin to use the emotions that are engendered by the client-professional relationship to learn more about the client. Freedberg suggests that:

> much of the time the practitioner is picking up on feelings the client
> is experiencing and cannot acknowledge. Once aware of these dynamics,
> he or she can be more empathic and responsive to the client's distress.

This research literature suggests it is similarly important for the practitioner to understand their own emotional response to the client and that 'the relational view of the countertransference includes anything that helps or hurts a therapist's ability to maintain a real connection with a client - to be truly present and truly aware' (Freedberg 2008).

This type of reflective practice has been described by Thompson and Thompson (2008) as being 'a highly skilled activity' that involves analytical self-awareness, critical thinking and communication skills. They highlight a range of aspects of organisational culture as being antithetical to the development and practice of such reflective skills, in particular unsupportive or anti-learning cultures that are focused on managerial concerns and underpinned by a rationalist approach and a target-driven philosophy to policy.

While a number of tools and strategies have been developed to enable individual practitioners to build their reflective functioning, supervision appears to be a central mechanism for facilitating 'effective oversight and review of practice.' It is now widely recognised that 'the quality of supervision available is one of the most direct and significant determinants of practitioners' ability to develop and maintain critical mindsets and work in a reflective way' (Burton 2009). One of the concerns raised by a number of commentators, however, is that the 'case management' function of supervision actually takes precedence over other functions (Burton 2009).

Burton highlights a number of forums that can provide the reflective space that is essential for good practice. These include co-working, consultation forums, group supervision and case discussions in allocation and team meetings, and the skilled use of external or child protection specialists. Other models include the complete separation of the managerial and reflective aspects of supervision (ie involving the use of a clinical supervisor in addition to a line manager), mentoring schemes for new staff and managers and the use of small teams (rather than a single worker) led by an experienced practitioner for each case. Case-file audits, both within agencies and across multiagency teams, are alsó being used to develop reflective practice. Perhaps most importantly, it is suggested that senior managers demonstrate their commitment to such working through the systems and processes that they encourage (Burton 2009) (see Box 2.8).

Box 2.8: Management contribution to reflective practice

'Managers should continuously work to promote an ethos of openness, rigour and challenge, as such environments are most likely to produce staff who routinely and effectively play their own "devil's advocate", using opportunities such as supervision, surgeries, consultation sessions, co-working and other forums or mechanisms to engage a "fresh pair of eyes".' (Burton 2009)

Ruch (2005) similarly suggests that 'anxieties, which arise from uncertain and risky situations, need containing not only for clients but for the practitioners as well'. Burton (2009) cites research that highlights the vital importance of the support role of supervision 'in helping front-line staff cope with the stress and anxiety generated by their work' alongside the need for workers to 'feel free to express their fears openly and with the confidence that they will be supported through supervision, without fear of such admissions being seen as not coping' (Burton 2009). Although we are still awaiting the implementation of Laming's (2009) suggested clarification to the General Social Care Council's Codes of Practice for Social Care Workers and Employers of Social Care Workers in terms of the quality and amount of supervision, and the amount of time allowed for reflective practice and support, the Social Work Task Force has now recommended monthly supervision for social workers (Social Work Task Force 2009).

Family-centred

The latter part of the twentieth century witnessed a radical shift in the way in which children and childhood were conceptualised, which in turn led planners and providers towards the development and provision of more 'child-centred' services. Based on the 1989 United Nations Convention on the Rights of the Child (Committee on the Rights of the Child 1989), children were recognised as having rights and entitlements, not least of which was the right to be actively involved in decisions about their future. It has been suggested, however, that the emphasis on the need for children's services to be child-centred has resulted not only in practitioners 'practising first and foremost in the interests of the child', but also often 'seeing the child's interests as potentially competing with those of the parents' (Bain 2009). Indeed, a study by Scourfield and Pithouse (2006) found that social workers perceived the child to be the client and that, consistent with government policy (Department of Health 2000), they did not 'perceive work with women and men, for its own sake, as part of their task', even though social work intervention in terms of both safeguarding and child protection involves working in partnership with parents (see above for further discussion of the limitations of the way in which this concept is being applied) and intervention is often targeted towards parents (Bain 2009).

It has also recently been suggested that although services are increasingly child centred, they are not yet 'infant centred' and that recent evidence about the extraordinary capacities of the infant for agency, coherence and affectivity (Stern 1998) requires a radical revision of our current conceptualisation of infants and a corresponding move towards more 'infant-centred' services, and indeed, infant-centred practitioners (Barlow and Svanberg 2009). The current absence of understanding on the part of a wide range of professionals working with children, about both the capabilities and needs of children during the first three years of life, results in many babies and toddlers experiencing parenting that constitutes a significant risk of harm, but which currently goes undetected unless the family is brought to the attention of children's services for other reasons (eg faltering growth or other measures of neglect).

The importance of being 'family centred' has been demonstrated by research showing that children's adaptation is primarily affected by the quality of relationships and interaction across a number of family domains. Cowan and Cowan (2008), for example, have highlighted five major domains of family life (Box 2.9).

Box 2.9: Five-domain family process model of the connections between risk factors and child outcomes

1. The quality of the mother-child and father-child relationships

2. The quality of the relationship between the parents, including communication styles, conflict resolution, problem-solving and emotion regulation

3. The patterns of both couple and parent-child relationships transmitted across the generations from grandparents to parents to children

4. The level of adaptation of each family member, his or her self-perceptions, and indicators of mental health and psychological distress

5. The balance between life stressor and social supports outside the immediate family. (Cowan and Cowan 2008)

The research underpinning this framework shows that it is the 'quality of relationships and the process of interactions within families that are central to the well-being of children', with attachment insecurity (see section on 'Social and emotional development' below for further discussion) playing a significant role in the intergenerational transmission of relationship problems (Cowan and Cowan 2008), and factors beyond the family creating a range of sources of stress or support. Research using sophisticated statistical modelling techniques, for example, suggests that parenting and the parent-child relationship actually mediate the impact of a range of other factors, including that of socio-economic status (Larzelere and Patterson 1990). This suggests that a focus on parenting and the parent-child relationship should be at the core of all intervention strategies.

While many prevention and treatment programmes target parental and family characteristics across multiple ecological domains, one concern that has been raised is that few interventions directly address the core relationship issues involved (Howe et al. 1999). This concern has increased in significance over the past decade because research that has emerged during this time has demonstrated unequivocally the importance of the early environment and, in particular, the period in-utero and during the first three years of life, in terms of all aspects of the child's later social and emotional functioning.[7] The importance of these factors will be discussed in more detail in Chapter Four.

Dyadic interventions

Over the past two decades, a range of interventions have been developed to address developmental problems in young children and mental health problems in the parent, with a view to promoting optimal child development. The former have primarily comprised behavioural programmes directed at helping the parent to develop new parenting skills, such as parent training programmes for example (eg Dretzke et al. 2009), and the latter have focused on parent counselling (eg Cooper et al. 2003).

[7] This is primarily because of the impact of early parenting on the child's developing brain. In maltreating families, parent-child relationships are characterised by hostility, low levels of reciprocity, engagement and synchrony, and by unpredictability (ie both ignoring, plus intrusive hostility). Research suggests a need to focus on family functioning and relationships (Cowan and Cowan 2008).

More recently a range of 'dyadic' interventions have been developed that are explicitly underpinned by a recognition of the 'bi-directionality' of the parent-baby/child relationship and the 'co-regulation' that takes place between them (Beebe and Lachmann 1987; 2005), and which point to the potential benefit of working with both parents and infants/young children together. Such approaches are typically underpinned by attachment or psychoanalytic theory and include interventions as diverse as video-interaction guidance, parent-infant/child psychotherapy, and some home-visiting programmes. A recent systematic review of the evidence found that such interventions can be highly effective in improving maternal sensitivity and infant attachment (Bakermans-Kranenburg et al. 2003). This is important given the increase in prevalence of early emotional abuse and neglect, and dyadic interventions of this nature have been found to be effective with emotionally abusive parents (Barlow and Schrader McMillan 2010).

Resilience/strengths-based

Resilience refers to the 'dynamic processes that foster positive adaptation in the context of significant adversity', as opposed to 'invulnerability' as is often thought (Walsh 2008). The research on resilience has attempted to address how or why it is that some individuals who suffer terrible traumas and daunting life circumstances, including growing up in extreme poverty, dealing with chronic medical illness, being severely abused or neglected, or experiencing catastrophic life events, trauma and loss, appear able to rise above such conditions and to lead a fulfilling life. One of the key findings of such research is that aspects of a positive mediating environment include the presence of at least one significant, positive, relationship, be it another parent, grandparent, teacher or mentor. The research also highlights the fact that resilience does not refer to a static set of traits that some individuals have and others don't have, but something for which there is potential throughout life, and that can be facilitated by more favourable environmental conditions and support (Walsh 2008).

A recent study exploring social workers' constructions of parenting, for example, and the way this 'feeds into' social workers' practice actions, found what is described as a 'surface static notion of parenting' in which the parent is, on the whole, viewed as being unresponsive and locked into their behaviours (Woodcock 2003). Personality is seen as a trait, and one that is unchanging over time. Problems are seen to be deeply ingrained and social workers are at a loss to know how to deal with this. They respond by seeking to get the person to change. It is suggested, however, that this view is inconsistent with the psychological and parenting literature, which suggests that parenting is a relationship and a task that fluctuates and also that it is determined by other psychosocial factors and relationships. Woodcock (2003) suggests that 'all-pervasive perceptions of this nature restrict the social worker's ability to respond positively to the needs of parents underlying their parenting'.

Walsh (2008) suggests that the conceptual move to a resilience or strengths-based model 'shifts the prevalent deficit-based lens from regarding parents and families as damaged and beyond repair, to seeing them as challenged by life's adversities with potential to foster healing and growth in all members'. She goes on to suggest:

> Rather than rescuing so-called 'survivors' from 'dysfunctional families' this practice approach engages distressed families with respect and compassion for their struggles, affirms their reparative potential, and seeks to bring out their best qualities. (Walsh 2008)

This type of approach is consistent with some of the other concepts discussed above (eg relationship and participatory practice) in that it involves focusing on engagement with the family via the professional's relationship with the client, and their use of skills and qualities such as respect and empathy. It is also consistent with the perspective of complexity and ecologically-situated families that function as complex adaptational systems, in which 'crises and persistent challenges impact the whole family and, in turn, key family processes mediate the adaptation of all members and relationships' (Walsh 2008).

The research strongly supports the use of strengths-based and resilience-focused approaches that are underpinned by the premise that people can rebound from serious trouble and adversity, and grow through dialogue and collaboration (Saleebey 1996). Increasingly, strengths-based approaches are being promoted as effective in the complex areas of statutory child protection work (Jack 2005). Within the context of resilience discourses, it is has been suggested that 'good outcomes for children are achieved through the promotion of positive parenting, stable family life, strong family and kin networks, community involvement and supportive social networks', and that the research 'reinforces the need to connect families to their wider family, social and cultural communities and positions the worker as an advocate for these ideals' (Connolly 2007).

User level

Transactional-ecological

A number of aetiological models of child abuse have now been developed and the most advanced of these recognise both the specific and heterogeneous risk factors associated with the occurrence of abuse, alongside the dynamic and reciprocal contributions made by the environment, child and parent in terms of a child's development (Cicchetti and Lynch 1993; Cicchetti and Carlson 1989). Within this model 'maltreatment is treated as representing a dysfunction in the parent-child-environment system rather than being solely the result of aberrant parental traits or environmental stress or deviant child characteristics' (Cicchetti and Carlson 1989). This model is underpinned by the recognition that a range of factors influence parental and family functioning (eg Belsky 1993; Cicchetti and Rizley 1981; Cicchetti and Carlson 1989) and thereby that 'parents and children function across multiple ecological domains with short- and long-term potentiating and compensatory factors nested within each of these ecologies' (see Box 2.10). This suggests that: 'At any given time the various ecological domains may interact catalytically, just as risk and protective factors may either ignite or buffer maltreatment at the various levels' (DiLillo, Perry and Fortier 2005). The term 'transactional' recognises that these exchanges or processes are bi-directional (two-way) as opposed to uni-directional (one-way).

Box 2.10: Ecological/transactional model (Cichetti and Carlson 1989)

Temporal dimension	Potentiating factors	Compensatory factors
Enduring factors	Vulnerability factors: Enduring factors/conditions increasing risk of harm	Proactive factors: Enduring factors/conditions decreasing risk of harm
Transient factors	Challengers: Transient but significant stressors	Buffers: Transient conditions which buffer stress

The implications of this conceptual model in terms of safeguarding practice is that it contributes to an understanding of the diverse factors involved in the development of a range of problems that may be experienced by families, and thereby the need to intervene across multiple systems at different levels in order to address such problems. This concept underpins the *Framework for the Assessment of Children in Need and their Families* (Department of Health 2000).

Social and emotional development

Children's maturation from infancy, through childhood, to adolescence and adulthood is characterised by a series of systematic biological, psychological and social changes. Knowledge about the development of children is now highly advanced, and research from a range of disciplines shows beyond question that the early environment, and the first three years of life in particular, play a major role in shaping children's cognitive, socio-emotional and behavioural development. The research that has emerged over the past decade has a number of seminal implications in terms of safeguarding practice, both as regards the need for much better early intervention, and also for the earlier removal of children when intervention is proving unsuccessful.

Specifically, recent research has shifted the emphasis away from children's cognitive development towards their social and emotional development, and the role that the early environment plays in terms of their ability to regulate affect and arousal. For example, it is now recognised that the most important aspect of the infant or toddler's early environment is the relationship they have with their early caregivers. This is because human infants are born with very immature brains that grow exponentially during the first few years of life, and the nature and quality of interactions with primary caretakers therefore play a significant role in both the neurophysiological and biochemical structuring of the brain (Schore 1994). For example, we now know that early experiences of persistent neglect and trauma can result in overdevelopment of the neurophysiology of the brainstem and midbrain (which can lead to anxiety, impulsivity, poor affect regulation and hyperactivity), and also to deficits in cortical functioning (ie problem-solving) and limbic function (ie empathy) (Gerhardt 2004). These findings disconfirm the popular conception that infants and toddlers are too young to be affected by abuse and neglect. Figure 2.2 shows the differences in brain development between a 'normal' three-year-old child, and one who has experienced extreme neglect.

There is also an extensive body of research concerning the role of 'attachment' in children's capacity to regulate their emotions. Attachment is now one of the best-researched concepts in the field of developmental psychology, and while there are still areas about which we need further research (Rutter et al. 2009), one of the most consistent findings is that up to 80 per cent of children raised in high-risk (ie abusive) environments have disorganised attachments (van Ijzendoorn et al. 1999). Children with disorganised attachments have considerable difficulty in regulating their emotions, and develop an 'incoherent autobiographical narrative', which is consistently found to predict a range of poor outcomes, including violence and aggression (eg Lyons-Ruth 1996) and serious psychological problems including personality disorders (ie narcissistic, antisocial, borderline and psychopathic disorders) (eg Steele and Siever 2010). This is due to the fear and trauma they have experienced at the hands of their primary caregivers and the development of highly negative and inconsistent internal working models. Neglect and trauma that occur during the first three years of life therefore have a significant and enduring impact on the later development of the child.

A number of aspects of early parenting (see Box 2.11 and for an overview see Barlow and Underdown 2008) have been identified as being particularly important during this period, and parents differ in their ability to provide these.

Figure: 2.2 Differences in the brain development following sensory neglect

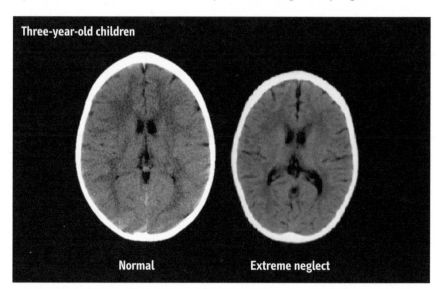

These images illustrate the negative impact of neglect on the developing brain.
The CT scan on the left is from a healthy three-year-old child with an average head size
(50th percentile). The image on the right is from a three-year-old child following severe
sensory-deprivation neglect in early childhood. The child's brain is significantly smaller
than average and suggests abnormal development of the brain (Perry 2002).

Most recently, Fonagy et al. (2003) have referred to the infant's need for a parent who
is capable of 'reflective function' (also known as 'mentalisation' and 'mind-mindedness')
and who can experience and respond to them as an 'intentional being' with their own
personality traits, strengths and sensitivities, rather than just in terms of their physical
characteristics and behaviour. Perhaps most importantly, it refers to an ability to
understand people's behaviour in terms of mental states.

Walker (2008) cites the work of Fonagy who provides the example of a three-year-old
child who sees his friend hide a piece of chocolate in a box and for which he says he
will come back later. However, the experimenter moves the chocolate to a different
location and then asks the three-year-old where his friend will look when he returns.
The three-year-old invariably suggests the new location, rather than the place in which
his friend actually hid it. An older child who has a better developed understanding
of mental states will not base his prediction on his own representation of reality,
but on his advanced understanding, which enables him to recognise that another
person's motivation, perspective or understanding may be different from his own -
in other words, that the internal and external may be different (Walker 2008).
However, individuals who do not receive the sort of parenting that enables them
to develop a capacity for reflective function are more likely to assume an 'equivalence
between what is internal and what is external' (Walker 2008).

> **Box 2.11: Key aspects of early parenting**
>
> > Sensitivity/attunement - the use of eye contact, voice-tone, pitch and rhythm, facial expression and touch to convey synchronicity with the infant
>
> > Mind-mindedness/reflective function/mentalisation - a parent's capacity to experience their baby as an 'intentional being' with their own personality traits, strengths and sensitivities, rather than just in terms of their physical characteristics and behaviour
>
> > Marked mirroring - happens when a parent shows a contingent response to an infant, such as looking sad when the baby is crying; the mirroring is marked in that it is sufficiently different from the infant's expression to indicate separateness, and thereby indicates that things can be made better
>
> > Containment - this occurs when a parent uses touch, gesture and speech to take on board the infant's powerful feelings and make them more manageable
>
> > Reciprocity - this involves turn-taking and occurs when an infant and adult are jointly involved in initiating, sustaining and terminating interactions
>
> > Continuity of care - provides infants with sufficiently continuous caretaking from a small number of key carers to enable them to become securely attached.

This emerging body of evidence has also resulted in an increased recognition of the benefit of what have been termed 'dyadic' methods of intervening (see above) to support parent-infant/toddler interaction.

Participatory

User participation was one of the key concepts underpinning *Working Together to Safeguard Children* (Department of Health, Home Office and Department for Education and Employment 1999). Bain (2009), however, suggests that participation through the active involvement of users and carers in the planning of services and tailoring of individuals' packages of care, as promoted in the white paper *Modernising Social Services* (Department of Health 1998), achieves only a degree of tokenism towards a goal of consulting with parents. We suggest throughout this publication that real participation is enabled through a model of partnership working, which involves a continual process of negotiation with clients and respectful recognition of their expertise. The concepts of participation and empowerment are linked with those of resilience and strengths-based approaches, which were discussed above.

Summary of findings

In this chapter we have introduced a range of concepts that are underpinned by extensive evidence and consensus opinion. The concepts apply at a range of levels (ie system, practitioner and user), and also across the full range of safeguarding services. Together these provide a coherent and comprehensive set of concepts to underpin a 21st century model of safeguarding (see Figure 2.3), and they will inform the discussion throughout the remainder of this publication.

Figure 2.3: Conceptual underpinnings of a 21st century model of safeguarding

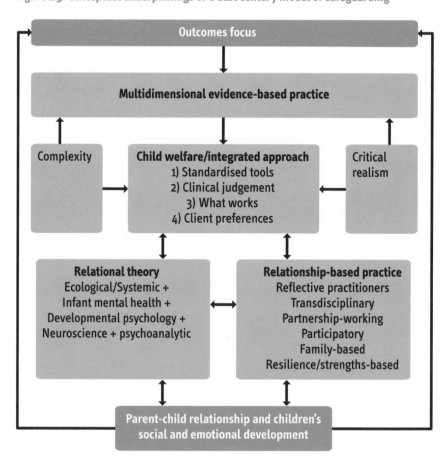

chapter three

Assessment of families

This chapter examines:

> recent findings with regard to the use of the Common Assessment Framework

> recent findings since the refocusing initiative with regard to the use of initial and core assessments

> recent evidence that emphasises the importance of assessing parenting capacity, parent-child interaction, and parental readiness and capacity for change.

3.1 Introduction

Child and family policy in the UK is focused on helping children to achieve good developmental outcomes by reducing social exclusion and providing both practical and emotional support at an early stage with the aim of preventing more long-term problems (Cleaver and Walker 2004). One consequence of this has been the need for a range of service providers to become involved in 'assessment' in order to 'identify accurately and sensitively those children who may require services' (Cleaver and Walker 2004).

The Common Assessment Framework (CAF/eCAF) is one part of a tripartite system (including also the ContactPoint database and Lead Professional), which was introduced to facilitate better outcomes for children (Garrett 2009) through the 'development of a culture of assessment, information sharing and earlier intervention amongst child welfare practitioners' (Pithouse et al. 2009). It is 'a tool to enable early and effective assessment of children and young people who need additional services or support from more than one agency', and comprises a 'holistic consent-based needs assessment framework which records, in a single place and in a structured and consistent way, every aspect of a child's life, family and environment' (Department for Children, Schools and Families 2010). It is directed at universal service practitioners (eg health, education, voluntary and private sectors) and is located firmly within the Every Child Matters agenda, which identified five outcomes that are key to well-being in childhood and later life - being healthy, staying safe, enjoying and achieving, making a positive contribution, and economic well-being (Department for Education and Skills 2003). It was piloted across a number of 'trailblazing' local authorities in 2005 with the long-term aim of being fully implemented in England by the close of 2008. It was intended that the CAF would help 'practitioners develop a shared understanding of a child's needs, so they can be met more effectively' and that it would 'avoid children and families having to tell and re-tell their story'; it was 'designed specifically to help practitioners assess needs at an earlier stage and then work with families alongside other practitioners and agencies to meet them' (Gilligan and Manby 2008). The CAF is not, however, a referral form (Department for Children, Schools and Families 2010).

The 'refocusing' initiative (see Chapter One), which was similarly based on the findings from a programme of research on child protection (Department of Health 1995) and a series of government inspections (Social Services Inspectorate 1997; Cleaver and Walker 2004), aimed to introduce a more holistic, multiagency approach towards the assessment of children in need. It was intended to move the focus away from the identification of abuse and neglect, which was 'incident driven', experienced by families as traumatic and intrusive, and rarely resulted in the provision of services unless abuse was substantiated.

'Assessment' was viewed as being one of the key processes involved in improving the lives of children and families in need of such support and services. *The Framework for the Assessment of Children in Need and their Families* (the Assessment Framework - Department of Health 2000) defines assessment as a systematic process of gathering a range of information relating to a child to help identify their strengths and needs in order to decide appropriate further action. It was viewed as providing a baseline of information against which a child and family's future development could be measured, and it recommends that the information be gathered from a wide range of sources. The broad principles underpinning assessment have been summarised in the Department for Children, Schools and Families' guidance on Every Child Matters and include being child or young-person centred, non-discriminatory, collaborative, continuous, progressive, transparent, consensual, current, sufficient and formative, and sound.

The tripartite focus of the Assessment Framework (ie on child development; parents and carers; and family and environment) is underpinned by a number of conceptual models. These include: 1) an ecological model that recognises the potential impact of the multiple ecological domains within which children and families are embedded and which serve as both protective and risk factors; 2) developmental theory that recognises the centrality of the child's attachment to the parent and its role within their later development; and finally 3) a partnership model of working.

The Assessment Framework identifies three assessment stages: referral, which is made by or on behalf of a child; initial assessment, which is a brief assessment of whether a child is in need (as defined by the Children Act 1989) and which services are required; and a core assessment, which is an in-depth assessment led by children's social services.

At the heart of all assessment processes at any stage of the safeguarding continuum is the need to make decisions in the face of uncertainties and incomplete information, and in often hostile and highly stressful contexts (Burton 2009). A recent review of the evidence concerning the oversight and review of cases in the light of changing circumstances and new information, concluded that while some practitioners persisted in initial judgements or assessments and showed a tendency to 're-frame, minimise or dismiss discordant new evidence', others responded to new information by abandoning their preferred view and 'jumping around from one item or theory to the next, never reaching a coherent conclusion or co-ordinated response' (Burton 2009). It is suggested that assessment should be an ongoing process, undertaken by practitioners who are adept in developing trusting relationships with children and families, thereby providing the basis for the development of deeper understanding about needs and circumstances (see Chapter Four). Burton also highlights the need for an organisational context that establishes the systems and ethos for the type of reflective practice that enables such decision-making (see Chapter Six).

This chapter examines recent research that has evaluated the implications of some of the policies referred to above, in terms of both practice and outcomes for children. It will suggest that while policy changes that have been developed over the last ten years have created a framework for the provision of a more effective model of safeguarding and one that is consistent with evidence about effective practice from European models, there is nevertheless a significant gap between such policy and practice on the ground. Specifically, the research suggests that despite early reservations about the value of the CAF (Laming 2003), findings point to its value in terms of a number of levels of outcome. However, there is a need for considerably more effort on the part of local authorities and Children's Trusts to fully embed the CAF process and integrated working (Burton 2009). The research also points to the need for further refocusing in terms of the use of initial and core assessments, which both maintains the integrity of the framework, and is also underpinned by research findings and the broader conceptual approaches highlighted in the previous chapter.

3.2 Safeguarding assessment

This section examines the most recent research findings with regard to the implementation and use of the CAF.[1] We also examine recent findings from the Local Authorities Research Consortium (LARC), which was established in 2007 to evaluate progress, to inform practice and to share findings and recommendations locally and nationally, using research. The first two LARC reports summarise the findings of work with local authorities about the use of the CAF and integrated working.

The Common Assessment Framework

Research on the implementation and benefits of the CAF is still very much in the early stages, and is wide-ranging in terms of its focus, including: the potential for cases to be addressed using the CAF (Mason et al. 2005); early versions of the CAF (Ward et al. 2002; Pithouse 2006); the factors helping or hindering practitioners in implementing the CAF/ Lead Professional working (Brandon et al. 2006); and the implementation of the CAF in England (Gilligan and Manby 2008; Peckover et al. 2009; Thorpe et al 2007; White, Hall and Peckover 2009) and in Wales (Pithouse et al. 2009; Pithouse 2006).

In terms of the classification of cases, Thorpe et al (2007) examined all new or re-referred case file records (235 children living in 160 families) for one social services department children and families assessment team during one month in April, classifying the cases into five categories (section 17 cases; section 47 cases; child concern reports; CAF cases; and section 17/CAF cases). The study found that education, health and police accounted for over 80 per cent of the referrals to social services, and that 'almost half of the cases currently being referred to children's services might potentially be diverted via a common assessment'. Furthermore, only a small proportion of these families actually received an additional resource or service as a result of the referral. The authors conclude that these findings point to the need for the broader children's workforce to change their philosophy on the use of the CAF from one in which such assessments are used to exclude children from their systems (ie by referring on to children's services) to one in which they use the assessment process to make joint decisions with families and other practitioners about the services and resources that are needed.

These results confirmed the earlier findings of Mason et al. (2005), who investigated the potential for cases to be dealt with outside formal service procedures and which type of cases could potentially qualify for a CAF assessment by examining case file records from all referrals made to children and families teams in Oldham during one month in 2003. They found that 49 per cent of referrals could have been classified as CAF cases and 'diverted via a common assessment to other forms of intervention' (cited in Gilligan and Manby 2008).

Despite the potential for assessment and referral by use of the CAF, the research also suggests such assessments are not being conducted. A recent study examined the CAF process in two northern locations over six months (Gilligan and Manby 2008). It found that despite a Department for Education and Skills estimate that around 20 to 30 per cent of children have additional needs at some point in their lives, and local estimates that between a quarter and a third of children and young people in the area could potentially benefit from a CAF assessment and the subsequent provision of services, only 26 CAF assessments had been completed over the six-month period.

---

1. It is beyond the remit of this review to address issues regarding the implementation of the Children's Integrated System.

Gilligan and Manby note that practitioner experiences of CAF assessments were that they had 'major resource implications as regards their time, and that they had little expectation that staffing resources would be increased as a result'. Although many practitioners recognised the local need, CAF assessments were regarded as being 'additional to their core activities'. Furthermore, the type of issues dealt with focused largely (90 per cent in one area and 60 per cent in the second) on concerns about children's behaviour. Other problems involved difficulties in including family members in the assessment process. Although 88 per cent of assessments had at least one parent or carer present during the assessment, only 28 per cent involved the young person, and even fewer assessments involved fathers. Gilligan and Manby also suggest that not only have CAF assessments been offered to a very small proportion of their potential beneficiaries, but that 'larger numbers would result more in the identification than the meeting of needs'. They conclude overall that small numbers of children and young people actually received the service; that despite genuine enthusiasm from practitioners for them to be so, the process observed could not yet be described as fully 'child centred'; that fathers are insufficiently involved; and that the CAF is, in reality, another service 'rationed' according to resources available and according to agencies' priorities.

The CAF appears, however, to have improved practice in terms of a number of factors. For example, a study in Wales found a decrease in missing basic background information, an increase in health-related information and the provision of more information about educational needs, as well as a greater emphasis in assessments on parent and family strengths (Pithouse et al. 2009). This study also found that the completion of a CAF assessment as a pre-condition for referring children with unmet needs had had the effect of reducing the overall number of referrals, although there was also evidence that they had 'triggered a more focused response from social services'. The CAF has also helped staff to develop a wider view of the child and family, and improved multiagency working and information sharing (Brandon et al. 2006).

However, reflecting on research conducted in England (Peckover et al. 2009; White, Hall and Peckover 2009), Pithouse et al. (2009) suggest there are in fact two CAFs: 'the "CAF of policy" which is the formal policy construct and the "CAF of practice" which is the applied CAF as constructed by multiple organisations across Wales and England, wherein there is no singular model'. They question the capacity for the CAF to be a coherent standardising medium for assessment because of a range of issues. These include lack of IT skills and resources, and the suggestion that the opportunity costs involved in operating the system are a 'time-consuming diversion from actually engaging with service users'. Consent and explicit participation of children is still low, and there is a predominance towards describing a 'concern' rather than a 'need'. They suggest that 'in short, there is little that is common in the way the CAF operates across England and Wales'. However, they also observe that the CAF is 'becoming the required system of preliminary assessment and referral'. In addition 'its rule is being extended to sectors previously without an assessment remit' and it is also replacing previous referral systems.

Although it is intended for use with children with additional needs rather than where there are concerns are about child abuse (Munro 2005), the CAF puts in place a mechanism by which universal-level practitioners can raise safeguarding concerns about children. For example, early evaluation across 12 pilot local authorities found that the common assessment process was effective in prompting social services to become involved (Brandon et al. 2006). However, despite these positive findings, research also showed that there was not always a good join-up between services for early intervention and safeguarding, and that children's need for protection could, as such, continue to go unnoticed (Brandon et al. 2006).

Research exploring the factors that help or hinder the implementation of the CAF (see Box 3.1) found anxiety about new ways of working and also about the increased workload generated, alongside a lack of support at managerial level (Brandon et al. 2006). It also found that the bulk of the CAF work is being undertaken by education and health professionals and that the holistic assessment of children requires new skills and ways of working, and is making new emotional demands on workers.

Brandon et al. conclude that a top-down, formal approach will work effectively if a number of criteria are met: i) a clear strategy for implementation; ii) awareness raising across the whole area; iii) a phased roll-out or a pilot, followed by quick implementation of both the CAF and Lead Professional at the same time; iv) multiagency training that includes operational managers; and v) a good IT system in place. They also point to the need for 'firmer national guidance about CAF and Lead Professional roles and processes', including a single nationally approved CAF form.

Box 3.1: Factors that help or hinder implementation of the CAF (Brandon et al 2006)

Factors that help implementation	Factors that hinder implementation
Enthusiasm at grass roots and managerial level	Lack of agency join-up and conflicts of interest
Perceived benefits for families	Lack of professional trust
History and practice of good multiagency working (including previous common assessment or Lead Professional)	Mismatch between the 'vision' and the practice
Learning from others	Confusion and muddle about processes
Existing IT system	Skill and confidence gaps
Clear structures for CAF/ Lead Professional process	Lack of support
Good training, support and supervision	Anxiety about increased workload
	Anxiety about new ways of working

As with much of the other research, Brandon and colleagues conclude that 'the work should be primarily about relationships rather than systems' and that multiagency working in itself doesn't improve outcomes for children, but needs 'a positive supportive climate within agencies' that promotes 'good relationships between practitioners and children and families'. They argue this is necessary to enable professionals to be seen as both available and responsive.

The CAF and integrated children's services

The Local Authorities Research Consortium (LARC) has undertaken two rounds of evaluation with local authorities (LARC1 - 2007/8 and LARC2 - 2008/9), to examine a range of process and outcome factors in relation to the use of the CAF to promote integrated children's services. LARC2 involved the collection of a range of quantitative and qualitative data from over 350 participants (ie parents and children in early years; Key Stage 3 non-attenders; and children and young people at risk of negative outcomes). Reports were submitted by the 24 participating LAs on the following issues: engaging children, younger people and families; the Lead Professional role; and Children's Trust arrangements (Easton et al. 2010). Figure 3.1 demonstrates the NfER impact model that was used to assess whether change had occurred. The model comprises four levels:

Level 1 impacts that relate to changes, inputs (such as the introduction of tools and frameworks), processes (such as the type of service offered, eg earlier intervention) and to service and management structures.

Level 2 impacts that involve changes to the experiences and attitudes of the key players within the services involved, ie practitioners and service managers. These impacts, which are dependent upon perceptual evidence, can also be considered 'soft' impacts.

Level 3 impacts that involve change to outcomes for the target population, ie children, young people and families in each of the three key groups (eg improvements in children and young people's emotional well-being, in family relations and in user experiences of services). These impacts include a number of related measures around each of the five Every Child Matters outcome areas.

Level 4 impacts that are the result of longer-term, more stable and embedded changes to the infrastructure, systems and processes within services, as well as more widespread sharing of practices and ideas (Easton et al. 2010).

Figure 3.1: Impact model (Easton et al 2010)

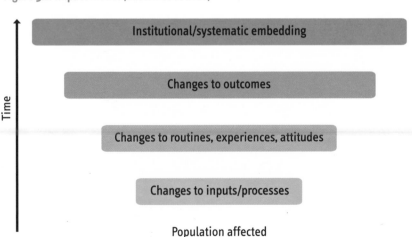

The results of the second round of data collection (2008/9) showed that at level 1 the impacts of the CAF process included enhanced engagement of children and families, better information sharing between agencies and multiagency professionals, the roll-out of targeted training programmes, the development of multiagency support teams, and the introduction of the CAF assessment as a single service request form for use by all agencies.

Level 2 impacts included increased use of the CAF when supporting families to move between universal and targeted services, increased numbers of multiagency professionals conducting CAF assessments, improved multiagency working through greater awareness of and trust between agencies, improved relationships between families and professionals, improved focus on the holistic needs of children and families, high levels of parental satisfaction with involvement in the CAF process, improved commitment to early intervention and prevention across most multiagency groups, and more positive experiences of multiagency professionals' involvement in the CAF process.

Level 3 impacts included examples of improved outcomes for children, young people, and families, as indicated by the local authorities' LARC research (see Box 3.2), by other local evaluation and monitoring procedures, and by use of the Children's Workforce Development Council's One Children's Workforce Tool (Easton et al. 2010).

Level 4 impacts of the CAF were limited, with some local authorities reporting that it was embedded in some areas of children's services only, although there was a strong commitment to further embedding. The authors suggest that more needs to be done both locally and nationally to ensure that longer terms impacts are recorded and monitored.

The LARC2 report also shows that most of the 24 authorities regarded themselves to be between levels two and three, with only a few authorities locating themselves at or between levels three and four in terms of integrated working (Easton et al. 2010). These findings suggest considerable progress between LARC1 and LARC2, but the authors conclude: 'More needs to be done locally and nationally to ensure the recording and monitoring of the longer-term impacts of early intervention and prevention, using the CAF process with children, young people and families'.

Box 3.2 summarises the ways in which the CAF is thought to be contributing to better outcomes for children. The report's findings also suggest improvements in outcomes for a number of other aspects of the CAF. For example, the initial assessment led to improved understanding of need; the Lead Professional role provided families with one point of contact alongside support; multiagency information sharing had led to an holistic understanding of need; and Team Around the Child meetings led to a more holistic understanding of need and appropriate referrals to services, alongside the implementation of targeted support interventions from a range of services and organisations working together.

Box 3.2: Contributions of the CAF process to child outcomes

Be healthy

Most local authorities provided evidence that the CAF process supported improvements to the emotional health of children, young people and families. In a small number of authorities, benefits extended to the physical health of children also. During the process (or post-CAF), local authorities reported children and young people had: improved behaviour; a greater self-esteem and confidence; a greater sense of responsibility and resilience; enhanced social and emotional awareness and enhanced general well-being, sometimes as a result of obtaining a medical diagnosis.

Stay safe

Local authorities found that through the CAF process, children, young people and families received a thorough needs assessment, which helped multiagency professionals identify individuals engaged in risky behaviours. Professionals were able, therefore, to provide families with a range of support mechanisms, which led to young people engaging in less risky behaviours and so to feel safe.

Enjoy and achieve

Local authorities reported that the CAF process enabled children, young people and parents to access appropriate support from multiagency professionals which then improved engagement in all aspects of school life, from greater attendance and learning to enhanced peer relations.

Make a positive contribution

Authorities' research showed that the CAF process helped children, young people and families to develop and improve relationships; it also empowered families and gave access to positive activities.

Achieve economic well-being

Authorities said the CAF process supported children, young people and families by improving their economic well-being, raising their aspirations for engagement in further education, employment or training, and addressing housing and welfare difficulties. (Easton et al. 2010)

The Framework for the Assessment of Children in Need and their Families

Early concerns that the refocusing of services away from child protection and in the direction of family support would reduce vigilance in relation to child protection (Millar and Corby 2006) were not substantiated. The results of the few available studies that explicitly addressed assessment practice since the refocusing initiative, suggested that not only is there no evidence of less protection for children, but that families valued this new approach (Platt 2001; Corby et al. 2002; Spratt and Callan 2004).

Early research (Platt 2001) found high levels of satisfaction from parents with the assessment and family support approach and 'very little evidence that the use of broadly based assessments where there are low-key concerns about a child's safety would be a dangerous form of practice'. Similarly, Corby, Millar and Pope (2002) examined parental perceptions about both initial and core assessments, and found that most parents appreciated initial assessments because they provided 'a speedy response, and were explicit and easily understood'. In addition, two-thirds of families were generally positive about the core assessments. The assessment process itself was seen by many as being beneficial and as providing opportunities for the ventilation of feelings and anxieties, and the clarification of communication about child protection concerns. When implemented with skill and sensitivity, it also 'helped create conditions in which some parents changed their attitudes to social workers, as well as to their own strengths and difficulties as carers'. Key factors in achieving the conduct of assessments that were felt by parents to be meaningful and helpful, even where child protection issues were the reason for social work involvement, included: 'the knowledge, skill and attitude of the assessor; an ability to tailor the standardised format to the individual situation; a willingness to listen carefully both to children and parents, and demonstrate empathy and respect; clarity about the specific purpose of the assessment; a positive belief in parents, ability to change'. Corby, Millar and Pope (2002) concluded that there was cause for cautious optimism about this new form of social work assessment.[2]

These findings were confirmed by later research involving a large survey of 24 English councils over a two-year period (866 initial and 86 core assessments), which found that three-quarters of parents reported very positive experiences. Councils had also found the Assessment Framework a success in terms of the involvement of children and families (Cleaver and Walker 2004).

Spratt and Callan (2004) similarly found that most social workers quickly addressed issues of risk before subsuming concerns with regard to such issues within the context of a full engagement with the family. They described this mode of working as 'covert surveillance/high engagement'. They also found evidence, however, of 'overt surveillance/ low engagement' where workers were interested in policing possible child protection risks with only perfunctory attempts to engage the family. The authors suggest that while the word 'risk' may have disappeared to some extent from the language of social work, it has not disappeared as a feature of social work practice. Rather, social workers have developed strategies for engagement with families that balance concerns about managing risk with concerns about meeting the family's welfare needs. The authors conclude, however, that the 'subtleties involved in such activity are not captured by official measures of governance, which concentrate more on indicators of performance'.

Platt (2006a; 2008) also found that initial assessments 'provide a form of practice that offers benefits in terms of balancing child protection and child welfare approaches, and in terms of relationships with parents'. She suggests that the use of appropriate safeguards, including satisfactory methods of facilitating a subsequent switching into child protection procedures where necessary, meant that initial assessments could be extended to include a wider range of cases. Platt notes, however, that an 'event focus' is still 'a defining factor in investigations', and that while initial assessments were viewed by social workers as being exploratory and having a less confrontational style, the process of 'investigation' was seen as requiring a 'forensic approach'. This suggests that in many cases, relationship and partnership-based working may be lost at the point where a concern about 'serious' risk of harm to the child predominates. This is of concern because it is not only antithetical to the model of safeguarding proposed here, but is actually the point at which partnership working is most needed.

Research that explicitly examined the potential of the new framework to be 'therapeutic' (Millar and Corby 2006) found evidence that it can be used therapeutically from the point of view of service users in terms of it being experienced 'as an enhancement to personal understanding or well-being', particularly when clients felt their views were respected and genuinely heard. Indeed, it was not only the skilful application of the form that was found to be beneficial but the format of the new framework itself.

2. Corby, Millar and Pope (2002) nevertheless raise concerns about the duplication of assessment, and repetition in the construction of forms, alongside the need to balance the needs of parents under stress and the needs of their children, and concerns about 'resourcing the framework's implementation'.

Millar and Corby conclude that such prescriptions for practice can be very helpful alongside social work expertise (including the flexible application of the assessment form). These findings confirm the suggestion that the 'distinction between assessment and intervention is unhelpful' in that it restricts 'the vision and creativity of social work staff' (Millar and Corby 2006), and point to the need to encourage practitioners to view the assessment process as having 'therapeutic' potential. The findings also point to the fact that assessment is the first step in what, for many families, will be a difficult process of developing a trusting relationship. Continuity of practitioner between assessments and family support is therefore important (see Chapter Four for further discussion).

However, the most recent study which addressed 'the dual functions of an integrated service in the light of a potentially widened mandate in line with recent policy changes', found some serious cause for concern. Hayes and Spratt (2009)[3] examined how social workers were continuing to manage this dual function 'by examining the ways in which social workers respond to child care problems (CCP)' (ie child welfare as opposed to child protection). This study found that social workers have 'responded to social policy goals to balance the protection of a lesser number of children whilst meeting the welfare needs of the greater by reducing the number of referrals designated child protection investigations (CPIs) and increasing the number of CCPs'. The authors suggest, however, that this involves 'a filtering system' to address perceived child protection risks within CCP cases, and that paradoxically, this results in closure of cases that are of more concern, with service provision largely confined to cases of least concern (see Box 3.3).

Box 3.3: Comparison of services for child welfare referrals where there are parent concerns (PC) and non-parent concerns (non-PC)

There was a notable difference between non-PC referrals and both single PC and multiple PC referrals and this was found to be consistent across the trusts. The majority of non-PC referrals received services (84.9 per cent, n = 62) whereas the majority of both single PC referrals (66.9 per cent, n = 83) and multiple PC referrals (65 per cent, n = 67) did not. It is also apparent that non-PC referrals received a higher mean number of services (1.51) than both single and multiple PC referrals (means = 0.44 and 0.69, respectively)', with the mean difference being statistically significant ($p < 0.005$). (Hayes and Spratt 2009)

This study found that 'the majority of non-parent concern referrals (ie child welfare/CCP) (55.1 per cent, n = 38) received two or more visits prior to case closure whereas the majority of both single and multiple-parent concern referrals received only one visit (61 per cent, n = 75 of single PC referrals and 63.3 per cent, n = 62 of multiple PC referrals)'. In over half of the cases, the reasons given for closure were 'that there were no concerns about the care of the children or that concerns had been "addressed" or "investigated" and not substantiated); only 16 per cent of cases had been closed following the provision of a service, the remainder having been closed because 'the families' difficulties had been resolved' (25 per cent).

Furthermore, the authors note that 'there was little sense of any systematic assessment taking place. Assessments were indicated in only one-third (n = 99) of all case files and in only just over one-third of these (n = 39) was any assessment documentation present, namely in only 13 per cent of all the case files examined'. This confirms the findings of the authors' earlier studies in which an assessment was noted in only 20 per cent of cases, and concern was expressed about the tendency of social workers to simply respond to problems presented.

3. This study was conducted in the Northern Irish Health and Social Services Trusts (equivalent to local authorities in England and Wales) and builds on the earlier work of Spratt (2001) and Spratt and Callan (2004).

Hayes and Spratt conclude that these findings can be reduced to the following equation:

We lack the necessary tools to adequately differentiate low and high-risk cases; because of collateral damage, it is politically and ethically unacceptable to route cases that appear to indicate lower risk through child protection processes; such lower risk cases are routed through child welfare processes; social workers must continue to manage risks inherent in child welfare cases; social workers achieve this by developing risk filtration practices; risk filtration practices inhibit the development of wider services to child welfare cases; paradoxically, child welfare cases bearing no perceivable risk are most likely to receive services. Result: the large majority of cases once conceived of as child protection but now as child welfare are processed through a risk filtration system. Policy aims with regard to preventative and service-orientated engagement are consequently subverted.
(Hayes and Spratt 2009)

These findings confirm those of an earlier study (Thorpe et al. 2007), which found that case file data categorised as section 47 and Child Concern Reports were more likely to be closed with no further action (72%) than those accepted as section 17 cases. Fewer services were offered to families who were assessed with a 'protective'/investigative orientation than those assessed with a 'child in need' orientation. The authors question whether section 47 referrals have fewer identifiable needs or whether the initial assessment is 'used differently depending on the reason for referral', thereby undermining the aims of the Assessment Framework to assess children and families 'according to the same needs irrespective of their presenting problems' (Department of Health 2000). Further analysis revealed that section 17 cases were twice as likely to accept the service offered compared with section 47 or CCP cases.

Thresholds

A number of studies have also examined the issue of thresholds with regard to the assessment process. Two studies examining the work of eight Area Child Protection Committees in England (Joint Chief Inspectors 2002; 2005) found that pressures on resources in children's social care were continuing to raise the threshold for services for children where there were concerns about their welfare (cited in Brandon et al. 2008).

A recent study (Platt 2006b), which examined local authority social workers' decision-making when considering referrals of children on the margin of child protection procedures, found that evaluation was based on five key factors - specificity (clarity and detail of the allegation); severity (degree of seriousness attached to the referral); risk (potential for and likelihood of future harm to a child); parental accountability (whether the parent might be responsible for harm); and corroboration (two types of corroboration - information about previous social services involvement, and referrals appearing in clusters with more than one referring agent providing similar information at the same time). These factors were used to determine whether to pursue an initial assessment or investigation. Cases that crossed the 'threshold' between no further action and initial assessment involved 'concerns about the wellbeing of a child: for which the parent could be held accountable; that could be interpreted as constituting a possible risk to the child; and that this evaluation was corroborated by other professionals or by previous social work involvement'. Cases that crossed the 'threshold' between initial assessment and investigation involved two further factors - 'either the specificity of reported harm to a child (eg an injury or specific allegation of sexual abuse); or the workers' interpretation of particular seriousness, based on either current information or a pattern that had emerged over time'. The factors tipping the balance towards investigation were specificity and severity.

Platt (2006b) suggests these findings confirm those of earlier studies (Giller et al. 1992; Wattam 1992), and that 'the use of these factors takes place in a climate of uncertainty' and is 'an integral feature of the referral stage, where information by definition, is limited and resources are stretched'. Furthermore, 'the use of a limited range of reasoning devices is a response to these circumstances', and is aimed at 'transforming uncertainty into a set of manageable decision-making tasks'. She also notes that it has been suggested that it is processes of this sort that lead to the child becoming 'silent' in social worker accounts (Platt 2006b), and that these findings confirm the event- or incident-driven focus of child protection procedures. Platt concludes that:

> in terms of our understanding of how to protect children, the concept of a simple continuum of abuse in which the level of a threshold is established on the basis of a scaling of degrees of abuse or neglect (Department of Health 1995), is no longer meaningful, and that a more holistic understanding of the child's circumstances is required.

More recently the first English study of a full cohort of serious case reviews commissioned by the Department for Children, Schools and Families (Brandon et al. 2008) showed that 'the preoccupation with thresholds was one of a number of interacting risk factors and many children's cases were on the boundaries of services and level of intervention'. By mapping 47 cases in terms of the level of services being received (ie level 1: universal; level 2: additional needs; level 3: complex needs and social services threshold of children in need; level 4: high risk, including child protection registration and regulated/restoratory services), the study found that just under half (n=21) were in receipt of level 1 and 2 services; of these, around a half were at the threshold for that level of service and 86 per cent of these children died. Similarly, of the 26 children who were receiving level three or four services, of whom 65 per cent died, a fifth were at the threshold for that level of service. Sixty-eight per cent (n=35/47) of these serious case reviews involved families described as low- or non-co-operative, and three-quarters (n=27/35) of these children died. The authors conclude that this spread of involvement of children across all level of services shows that staff delivering early intervention are working 'within the safeguarding continuum, and not in a separate sphere of activity', and that effective early intervention will be successful in identifying early risks of harm, some of which will require referral to children's social services. They suggest that lack of parental co-operation with appointments perceived to be necessary to safeguard the child's welfare or safety should be taken into account as part of the assessment process. As in continental Europe, it should be used to justify compulsory intervention or, indeed, to justify the involvement of more formal court-based systems (Scottish Executive 2002).

Brandon and colleagues' review of serious cases also found that 'the emotional impact of working with hostility from violent parents and working with resistance from older adolescents impeded engagement, adjustment and safeguarding action'. For example, they found evidence to show that one way of dealing with 'overwhelming information and the feelings of helplessness' generated in workers by such families is the 'start again syndrome' in which knowledge and information about the past are put away in order to focus on the current circumstances, particularly where there is a new pregnancy or new baby, and the chance for a fresh start.

Brandon et al. (2008) also found that many of the hard-to-reach young people who had experienced long-term, high-intensity, level three or four services who died as a result of suicide, did so at a point at which services were being withdrawn or scaled down. They suggest that 'these vulnerable and hard-to-help young people need more creative, more responsive, individually tailored services that extend into their adulthood and which can address root causes and not just respond (or fail to respond) to their distress' (see Chapter Four for further discussion about effective interventions). They also suggest that if these young people are returned home, both the young person and their parents or carers require a high level of support and not a minimal service. The recent *Lancet* review (MacMillan et al. 2009) found that once children have been placed in out-of-home care there is an assumption that reunification is the optimum outcome, yet the findings show that although up to 75 per cent of children are reunified, up to 40 per cent subsequently re-enter foster care. Moreover, this review suggests that reunified youth have worse outcomes in terms of internalising and externalising problems, risky behaviours, competencies, grades, school drop-out, involvement in the criminal justice system, adverse life events and witnessing physical violence (MacMillan et al 2009).

Brandon and colleagues suggest that the critical thinking required to enable staff to 'understand cases holistically, complete analytical assessments and weigh up interacting risk and protective factors' requires 'not only more resources but effective and accessible supervision' (see Chapter Four for further discussion).

Assessment and the prediction of risk

Recent research by Dorsey et al. (2008) found that although assessments of risk were associated with some of the factors that have been shown to predict the recurrence of maltreatment, overall, 'assessments were only slightly better than guessing'. Their study examined the factors associated with caseworkers' assessment of the risk of maltreatment recurrence among families in contact with social services and their subsequent reports of maltreatment. It found 'a complex picture of risk assessment in which there were few patterns of risk factors (other than prior reporting) that were consistently associated with caseworker classification of risk and subsequent report'. It also found that the correspondence between the assessment of risk and subsequent reports of maltreatment was low, and that there was greater accuracy for low- than high-risk cases. Although Dorsey and colleagues conclude that 'considerable improvement in risk assessment is needed so that at-risk families can be better identified and limited services available can be directed towards those most in need', we argue that this evidence confirms the suggestion that the prediction of risk is no longer a supportable activity. In accordance with some of the concepts described in Chapter Two (eg complexity theory, multidimensional evidence-based practice), we argue that structured clinical decision-making and indicative assessment is better supported by the evidence, and that more refocusing is required to move away from the 'detection of abuse' and towards the provision of effective intervention.

Other studies of the accuracy of the assessment process also found problems. Corby (2003) for example, found 16 per cent of 400 cases had an 'anomalous outcome' in the sense of there having been less or more child protection than would have been expected using an evidence-based set of weighted indicators. Cases in which less child protection services were provided than would have been expected mostly involved families experiencing multiple material and stress-related problems, all of whom were re-referred; most involved families with children under school-age; and most involved domestic violence or drug/alcohol misuse. No consistent follow-up or ongoing work was provided in any of these cases. Cases in which more protection was provided than would have been expected all resulted in child protection conferences; most resulted in non-registration; and the small number where help was needed did not require registration. Corby (2003) suggests that the use of a weighted instrument such as the one developed for the purposes of this research could be used to monitor whether the decisions that safeguarding teams are making are 'placing the right emphasis on safeguarding and support'.

Structured decision-making

A recent review (OXPIP 2005) of pre- and post-birth assessments for Oxfordshire Health and Social Care that involved talking to social workers before and after visits, highlighted the fact that few social workers used the Assessment Framework regularly or to its full potential. While newly qualified social workers were more inclined to use it, and liked its guidance and clarity, more experienced workers felt that it 'misses the point' and that the questions didn't encourage social workers 'to explore and develop ideas with parents'. The more experienced social workers felt the headings of the assessment were 'helpful as a guide', but tended to rely on 'previously acquired interviewing skills to lead their questions and assessment'. They felt 'the core assessment reduced the quality of information into standardised tick-box responses, which restricted rather than enhanced the end report' and one view was that 'the assessment framework does not cover the capacity of parents to change or their ability to be insightful about their previous behaviour'. The report notes that none of the social workers used any of the recommended standardised tools, although one reported she had done so in the past, and another found the ecomap useful with some families.

The findings of our review suggest that the rejection of the use of standardised tools of this nature by practitioners is no longer supportable, and that a structured assessment process is now called for. Assessment of families can be undertaken using clinical judgement or through the implementation of one of two types of assessment instrument: consensus-based models (ie tools comprising criteria based on clinical judgement) and actuarial-based models (tools developed through the use of empirical research to identify the risk factors and including some assessment of their predictive validity) (White and Walsh 2006). Research suggests that actuarial approaches are more accurate than either consensual approaches or the use of clinical judgement alone, particularly as regards the 'classification' of families at risk for child maltreatment (White and Walsh 2006). However, although actuarial approaches appear to be the most effective, they too are not completely accurate. Common problems include the fact that they tend to focus on a limited number of risk factors, and their limited generalisability to other times and populations. These findings point to the value of what has been defined as 'a third generation' approach which consists of 'empirically validated, structured decision-making' or 'structured clinical judgement' (White and Walsh 2006) (see Box 3.4).

> **Box 3.4: Structured assessment of risk**
>
> This approach attempts to bridge the gap between the scientific, actuarial approach and the clinical practice of risk assessment. The emphasis is on developing evidence-based guidelines or frameworks that promote systemisation and consistency yet are flexible enough to account for case-specific influences and the context in which assessments are conducted. Such instruments can promote transparency and accountability yet encourage use of professional discretion and are based on sound scientific knowledge but are practically relevant. (White and Walsh 2006)

Similarly, Shlonsky and Wagner (2005) highlight two distinct processes of assessment (see Figure 2.1): an assessment of the possibility of future harm, and a contextual assessment of child and family functioning used to develop case and intervention plans. They argue that both are critical decision aides but suggest there has been confusion in the field about their respective uses. Actuarial assessment instruments clearly have the greatest potential to reliably and accurately estimate the recurrence of child maltreatment, but many do not in fact have good predictive validity. Furthermore, actuarial risk assessment does not indicate which clinical factors are most important to address and which services are most likely to be effective. They point to the need for a structured decision-making approach.

3.3 What should the focus of assessments be?

The focus of assessment has been defined by the tripartite focus of the Assessment Framework (the development of the child; parents and carers; family and environment). This structure is underpinned by an ecological framework that recognises the significance for children of the broader context within which they are located, and the impact on them of a range of factors, such as parental mental health problems, drug/alcohol misuse and domestic violence. It also recognises that broader stressors, such as poverty and housing problems, can impact negatively on parents and on parenting practices. The focus of assessment should thereby take account of a wide range of issues.

However, both the conceptual framework developed in Chapter Two and the research identified by this review suggest that the parent-child relationship and parenting capacity should be at the core of the assessment process and that the focus should be on 'the sensitivity and responsiveness of parental behavior in the context of their interaction with the child' (Tarabulsy et al. 2008). The following three sections of this chapter examine this in more detail, looking in turn at assessing:

> parenting capacity

> parent-child interaction

> parental readiness and capacity to change.

Assessing parenting capacity

Although a number of systematic approaches to the assessment of parenting have been identified (eg Gray 2001; Azar et al. 1998; Browne 1995) these focus on the 'quality of parenting' and not the 'prime task of parenting' (Donald and Jureidini 2004). For example, Donald and Jureidini suggest that the *Framework for the Assessment of Children in Need and their Families* consists of 20 dimensions grouped across three domains, and that this results 'in a grouped list of factors with no indication of the relative importance of particular dimensions or how they interact'. The approach Donald and Jureidini adopt focuses on similar domains and has a similar definition of 'parenting capacity', however it differs in the emphasis it gives to such capacity, focusing on 'the adequacy of the emotional relationship between parent and child'.

Box 3.5 shows the key factors that Donald and Jureidini suggest are central to an assessment of parenting. They discuss the way in which parents are currently assessed as being above or below a 'threshold' in terms of parenting being good enough or otherwise, alongside the prevalence of adverse factors identified in the parents. They express concern about the tendency to downplay the significance of adverse parental factors when the child is identified as being difficult to parent. For example, there is often tolerance to a higher number of risk factors in the parenting domain when a child has been diagnosed as having ADHD. Rather than up- or down-grading adverse factors identified in the three domains, they suggest it would be more useful to incorporate them into an assessment of parenting capacity, thereby allowing a more 'reliable identification of those parents whose children must be considered to be at an unacceptable risk of experiencing further harm, independent of how challenging the child is'.

Box 3.6 identifies the keys steps involved in such a process. Donald and Jureidini suggest that a detailed discussion with parents about their harmful behaviour should identify the extent to which the parents 'have the capacity to see the experience from the child's point of view and to realistically appraise what might need to change for the child to thrive in their care'.

Box 3.5: Factors to be considered in assessing parenting

1. Primary domain: parenting capacity
Capacity to form healthy, intimate relationships, as manifest by:

> recognition of the child's needs and to put them before parental needs/wants

> awareness of the potential effects of relationship stresses on children

> ability to take responsibility for personal behaviour, including the abuse

> capacity to avoid dangerous, impulsive acts

> acceptance by the abusive parent of their primary responsibility for providing a safe environment for their child

> awareness by the parent[s] of the effects of their own experience

> provision of physical and emotional care appropriate to the child's developmental status

2. Modulating effects: child's parentability

> Any disability, illness or emotional disturbance either prior to, or as a result of maltreatment

> Degree to which the child's emotional state has been compromised by the maltreatment. This will be influenced by the child's pre-existing well-being and developmental status, the nature and frequency of the abuse involved and the relationship between the child and the abuser

> Developmental age of the child at the time of the abuse

> Any idiosyncratic meaning that a particular child might have to a caregiver

3. Modulating effects: scaffolding for parenting

> Knowledge base and parenting experience

> Support that parents are able to give each other in parenting

> Support or distress from extended family and other external sources

> Use of alcohol and other drugs

> Financial stresses

> Positive and negative effects of involvement in the legal system

> Relationship between parents and professionals (past and present), including readiness to accept professional help, and responses to previous professional attempts to help. (Donald and Jureidini 2004)

Box 3.6: Process summary of key stages in an assessment of parenting capacity, where abusive parenting has been identified

1. **Confirmation by a statutory agency of harm due to abuse**

2. **Establish carers' initial level of: acceptance that harm has occurred; and responsibility taken for harm**

3. **Conduct parenting assessment that establishes parenting capacity**

4. **Elicit carers' response to the negative aspects of parenting capacity**

5. **Gauge the influence of the assessed parenting capacity on the carers' level of acceptance of responsibility for harm (as defined in Step 2)**

6. **Provide a final opinion which:**

> reiterates the established harm

> states the initial level of responsibility taken by the carers for the harm done

> states the assessed parenting capacity and the consequential carers' response

> states the subsequent level of responsibility taken by the carers for the harm done to the child

> states the optimal management plan for the child[ren] and family in relation to future safety, therapeutic needs and reunification based on the assessment of parenting capacity, the level of responsibility taken by the carers and their preparedness to address the identified parenting issues.
(Donald and Jureidini 2004)

Donald and Jureidini provide the following case study to illustrate their point:

A young infant was admitted with a fracture dislocation of one elbow and several metaphyseal fractures. No explanation was proffered to account for the injuries, which were judged to be inflicted. A 'standard parenting assessment' which surveyed the three domains (parental factors, child factors and environmental factors) failed to identify the presence of any major adverse factors in any of the domains. The parents were well educated and had good supports, and the child had no handicaps. When the injuries were reviewed with the parents, the child's father was clearly distressed, seeking reassurance that the pain resulting from the fractures would not affect the baby long-term. However, the mother seemed not to share his reaction, only expressing concern as to what disease the baby must have to cause such fractures. Further careful exploration failed to identify any capacity for the mother to feel what it must have been like for the baby. Thus, while the 'standard assessment' did not identify any grounds for concern, we concluded from the mother's lack of empathy for the baby, that her ongoing care of the infant, in the context of the unexplained inflicted injuries, would continue to expose the baby to high risk of further harm.

Assessing parent-child interaction

The evidence points to the need for assessment to include an evaluation of parent-child interaction, and suggests that this is currently poor, particularly in terms of early parent-infant/toddler interaction. For example, the OXPIP review (2005) (referred to above) highlights the need for further training and support in the use of observation to assess the parent-infant/toddler relationship and to make sense of what is being observed. The report also highlights the need for further training and support in a number of other areas including the basics of infant and toddler development, how to apply attachment theory in practice, the use of geneograms, how to read non-verbal behaviour of a baby to provide clues about the parent-infant relationship, and ways of addressing negative feelings without jeopardising the client-worker relationship.

Consistent with the overall approach that is being recommended here (ie structured clinical judgement involving a combination of both standardised tools and clinical skills), parent-infant/toddler interaction should be assessed routinely by social workers who have received specialist training, or by a specialist professional such as a parent-infant psychotherapist. A range of standardised tools should be used as part of this assessment, of which the CARE Index (Crittenden 1981) is possibly the best example. It has been shown to differentiate abusing from neglecting, abusing-and-neglecting, marginally maltreating, and adequate dyads. It enables trained practitioners to observe (ideally using three minutes of videotaped parent-infant/toddler interaction) seven aspects of behaviour assessing affect, cognition and interpersonal contingency. It provides assessments of sensitivity, control and unresponsiveness for the adult; co-operativeness, compulsiveness, difficultness and passivity for the infant (birth to 15 months); and co-operativeness, compulsiveness, threateningly coercive and disarmingly coercive for the toddler (15 to 30 months). This assessment provides the practitioner not only with an indication of the severity of the problems, but also the type of intervention needed. For example, it is suggested that scores of 5 or 6 (out of 14) indicate the need for parent education; 3 or 4 the need for a parent intervention; and 0 to 2 the need for parent psychotherapy and child protection procedures. Crittenden observes that the need for and nature of the intervention should be based on the use of the CARE Index as part of a broader assessment of functioning, and recent research points to the value of such tools when they are conducted as part of a broader procedure for assessing parents' capacity for change (see Chapter Four).

In addition to the existing tools recommended by the Assessment Framework, OXPIP recommends the use of MORS (Mother-Object Relations Scale, which is a brief 14-item instrument indicating a representation of the baby in the mother's mind) and PIRGAS (Parent-Infant Relationship Global Assessment Scale) as possible additional tools. A range of other standardised tools of this nature are also available (eg Ages and Stages) and clinicians should have a wide range of these instruments available to them for selective use as required, as part of an evidence-based approach to practice (Austin 2009).

Assessing parental readiness and capacity for change

The research also suggests that in addition to a greater focus on parenting, there is a need to assess both readiness and capacity for change. Research assessing the predictive validity of 'problem recognition', 'intentions to change' and overall 'readiness for change' among primary caregivers in receipt of in-home services following substantiated reports of child abuse or neglect, showed that initial problem recognition and intentions to change predicted 'a few improvements in individual and family functioning, along with significant reductions in the likelihood of additional reports of child maltreatment within one year' (Littell and Girvin 2005). The researchers also found that initial intentions to change were predictive of reductions in the substantiation of subsequent reports of maltreatment. Although the overall measure of readiness for change was found to predict reductions in the likelihood of out-of-home placement, the authors conclude there were few advantages of an overall readiness score.

Littell and Girvin point, however, to the need for caution. They note that although such constructs can be assessed to some extent and predict some changes in individual and family functioning, and subsequent maltreatment, there is no causal association between the strength of constructs such as intentions to change and later outcomes (eg higher levels of problem recognition and intentions to change do not necessarily predict better outcomes). Furthermore, they suggest that assessment of problem recognition and intentions to change may have affected caseworkers' responses and may also have influenced subsequent patterns of service delivery, and that these may in turn have influenced outcomes. They suggest, therefore, that these constructs should not be used to predict who is most likely to benefit from treatment, but as an indication of the issues as part of a broader assessment process.

Further research by Littell and Girvin (2006) sets out to identify individual, family and caseworker characteristics associated with problem recognition and intentions to change in a sample of caregivers receiving in-home child welfare services following a substantiated report of abuse or neglect. It found that 'readiness for change may depend on the nature of presenting problems and the contexts within which these problems occur'. The authors argue:

> Since many caregivers face multiple problems, their recognition of salient issues and ability to address these issues may be quite uneven across problem domains. Caregivers may recognise and handle intrapersonal social, economic and environmental problems in different ways, and caregivers should not therefore be pigeonholed into global stages or categories of readiness to change.

Littell and Girvin go on to suggest that a more nuanced and potentially helpful approach to problem recognition involves what Leventhal et al. (1997) refer to as the 'problem domain' as the client views it, and that this involves the client's understanding or assumptions about the nature, causes, course and potential remedies for a given problem. Their findings also suggest that intentions to change are complex and should not be confused with willingness to work with a particular social worker or participate in a particular programme. Littell and Girvin's research points to the need for practitioners to conduct careful assessments of caregivers:

> views of the presenting problems

> goals and values

> levels of discomfort with the status quo

> hopes about whether the situation can improve

> views of available alternatives.

This is consistent with the partnership and participatory approaches referred to in Chapter Two.

It has also recently been suggested that 'cross-sectional assessment of families provides important information about family functioning at one point in time, but is of limited usefulness when the results are equivocal' (Harnett 2007), and that what is actually needed at such times is an assessment of a family's actual capacity to change, including an evaluation of the parent's motivation and capacity to acquire parenting skills. Harnett suggests this should include a number of steps (see Box 3.7).

These findings indicate that, as with the assessment process, an assessment of the family's capacity to change and evaluation of whether such change has taken place, should involve not only clinical judgement but also the discriminate use of a range of available standardised instruments.

> Box 3.7: Procedure for assessing parents' capacity for change in child protection cases

> 1. A cross-sectional assessment of the parents' current functioning, including the use of a range of standardised psychological tests to supplement other sources of information and to include an assessment of parent-child interactions.

> 2. Specification of operationally defined targets for change that should include the unique problems facing individual families and using standardised procedures such as Goal Attainment Scaling - GAS.

> 3. Implementation of an intervention with proven efficacy for the client group that addresses multiple domains of family functioning, is delivered in the home using individualised goals and is tailored to address the specific problems of individual families and the achievement of identified targets for change.

> 4. Objective measurement of progress over time including standardised tests administered pre and post the intervention; direct observation of changes in parent-child interaction; and evaluation of the parents' willingness to engage and co-operate with the intervention and the extent to which targets were achieved. (Harnett 2007)

Summary of findings

The CAF

> The research suggests that the CAF comprises a highly acceptable process to families that appears to benefit both service providers and users, but that it is currently seriously underused - and, where it is being used, it is often not being implemented as was intended.

> The CAF would appear to be the primary mechanism for linking the different service tiers in terms of safeguarding concerns, but is not currently fulfilling this role.

> There is a lack of national guidance about the CAF and Lead Practitioner roles, including the absence of a single nationally approved CAF form.

> Factors that facilitate its use include enthusiasm at grass roots and managerial level, perceived benefits for families, a history and practice of good multiagency working (including previous common assessment or Lead Professional), learning from others, an existing IT system, clear structures for CAF/Lead Professional process, and good training, support and supervision.

> Further changes needed locally include:

>> ensuring that practitioners have not only received multiagency and ongoing training in the use of the CAF and Lead Professional, but have also received training in partnership working (see Chapter Four) that provides them with the skills not only to undertake a participatory assessment process, but also to undertake 'therapeutic' working with families

>> some form of case-based supervision for staff involved in undertaking assessments (if they are not already routinely in receipt of supervision as part of their work)

>> workload allowances to be made for practitioners, in which workloads are reconfigured to allow for the increased demands made by this work, particularly in the short term

> ensuring that staff have access to appropriate IT systems
> ensuring that the responsibility and funding for Lead Professional work is shared across agencies.

Initial and core assessments

> Initial and core assessments are highly acceptable to many families and include positive experiences and involve the parent/children feeling 'involved'.

> Skilful application of these assessments enables them to be used 'therapeutically' with some families, which raises further questions about the legitimacy of drawing a distinction between assessment and intervention.

> Although early findings point to a good balancing of child protection and family welfare concerns with effective 'switching' as part of this process (defined as 'covert surveillance/high engagement'), recent findings suggest that a 'large majority of cases once conceived of as child protection but now as child welfare are processed through a risk filtration system', the consequences of this being early closure of cases that are of more concern, and service provision largely confined to families in which there is an absence of parent concerns.

> An 'event focus' is still the defining characteristic of 'investigations', with a corresponding loss of partnership/participatory working alongside other potential benefits.

> A pressure on resources continues to raise the thresholds for access to children's services and nearly half of families assessed do not receive a service.

> The correspondence between a positive assessment of risk and subsequent cases of maltreatment is low, supporting the shift of focus away from prediction and towards the use of indicative assessment.

> The evidence supports the use of an integrated model of assessment that combines the use of actuarial risk assessment with the application of clinical skills and judgement alongside the use of evidence about what works and client preferences.

> The assessment process is frequently seen as being an end-in-itself, rather than the first step of a multi-stage process aimed at assessing the level of services needed (as opposed to whether such services are required).

> Effective supervision is perceived as being a key part of the effective assessment of families.

> The implementation of an assessment process without the provision of supportive services to address the concerns raised may be experienced by families as having exacerbated their problems. This raises the possibility that the conduct of comprehensive assessments of this nature, without the offer of services, could actually be harmful to families.

> Lack of co-operation on the part of families is a key factor preventing effective assessment and needs to be included as a key indication of risk in the assessment process. Lack of co-operation should be used to justify compulsory intervention.

The focus of assessment

> There is currently little recognition in the assessment process of the importance of pregnancy and the first few years of life in terms of a child's functioning and later well-being, particularly the impact of the early environment (ie parenting) on the child's attachment and developing neurological system.

> There is a lack of expertise in relation to child development, particularly in terms of the use of validated and standardised tools (eg CARE Index) to assess parent-infant/child interaction, and of understanding the implications of what is observed.

> Many of the available standardised tools that are recommended as part of the Assessment Framework are not being used by experienced social workers, who perceive them to be part of a 'tick-box' culture.

> Practitioners should have access to a wide range of standardised tools that they use as part of the clinical decision-making process.

> All assessments should routinely include an evaluation of i) parenting capacity; ii) parent-infant/child interaction; iii) parental readiness and capacity for change.

> Other factors that need to be taken into account in terms of whether a child protection plan is put in place, are not only the level of problems identified by the integrated team, but also the parents' recognition and acceptance of the problem, their willingness to change and an assessment of whether change has occurred following the implementation of an intervention (see Chapter Four).

Chapter Six presents some recommendations in terms of the changes that are still needed in terms of policy and practice on assessment.

chapter four

How do we intervene effectively with families?

This chapter:

> considers how we should be supporting multi-problem families to change their behaviour by examining what is known about 'what works'

> examines evidence-based models of 'partnership' and 'relationship-based' practice as the core features of all intervention strategies, and discusses what such practice should involve

> examines the evidence about 'what works' to improve the parent-child relationship and parenting practice where there is concern about the abuse of (i) children under four, and (ii) older children

> discusses the importance of assessing parents' capacity to change within the context of the services being provided and ways of assessing whether the desired change in parenting has taken place.

4.1 Introduction

One of the key components of safeguarding practice is intervening effectively to bring about change in families experiencing complex problems, and the research suggests that expectations on this front are currently too low. Many children and families receive a plethora of services that don't meet stringent criteria in terms of 'effectiveness' and are therefore often not rated as being of value, and there is a significant gap in the evidence base in relation to how to intervene with more 'complex' cases at later stages of the problem (Brandon and Thoburn 2008). Indeed, there is some suggestion that the most 'complex', most 'challenging families' are those least likely to be helped by the programmes that emerge from systematic reviews as being effective (Utting, Monteiro and Ghate 2007).

These issues are compounded by a range of other factors. For example, one study that involved both clients and social workers found that the process of intervention was affected by a process of 'disculpability' in which each group blamed the other when interventions ran a negative course. What was termed 'adequate impotence' reigned supreme because each party felt unable to promote good relationships or efficacy, with each blaming the other for the outcomes, and both parties feeling that the outcome didn't really depend upon their actions (Sousa and Eusebio 2007).

There is increasing recognition that the practitioner/service-user relationship currently emphasises 'legal and administrative requirements and tasks and outcomes (Howe 1997), as opposed to the professional relationship and emotional aspects of an individual's circumstances', and that practice is dominated by 'procedural and managerialist responses' (Ruch 2005). There is also increasing recognition that 'under certain circumstances the child protection system can be harmful, specifically when statutory involvement acts to disempower parents and fails to specify or acknowledge changes that the family need to make to achieve a minimal standard of parenting' (Harnett and Day 2008).

The training of a range of practitioners over recent years, including social workers, has resulted in the development of a safeguarding workforce who are reluctant to 'engage in the often messy and uncertain intricacies of relationship-based practice with service users and their networks', and who feel a need to 'take cover behind the seeming certainty that procedure-led or "surface" approaches (Cooper and Lousada 2005) to their work might offer' (Ruch 2005). In the case of social work, it is suggested that this is largely due to the adoption of a pragmatic approach to the knowledge base of social workers (ie based on the National Occupational Standards, which is non-prescriptive in terms of the type of theories that should be used to inform practice - Ruch 2005), and the implementation of a training curriculum that 'starts from the practice context' and brings in theories, models and methods of working 'only when they help to make sense of the complexities of practice' (Hingley-Jones and Mandin 2007).

In Chapter Two we suggested that the use of relationship-based practice in social work has been influenced by a range of socio-political factors, not least of which has been the need for practitioners to develop a model of practice consistent with its underlying values. The move away from such relationship-based practice has, in part, been a reaction to the desire to work systemically (and to what is described by Walker (2008) as 'a residual view in some circles that it is oppressive to make use of psychotherapeutic knowledge and skills; as though by employing these ideas the worker necessarily forgets the impact on service users of wider social processes of discrimination and disadvantage') and, more recently, to wider managerial processes that have undermined the basis for such practice.

The focus of this chapter is on what the evidence suggests about intervening effectively to safeguard children from harm. We examine what the research suggests in relation to how we should be supporting 'multi-problem' families to change their behaviour, and what organisational strategies need to be in place to facilitate such practice. We will suggest that the answer to working effectively with families in which there is concern that a child is being harmed, lies not in the whole-sale adoption or implementation of evidence-based manualised programmes; rather, such programmes need to be implemented as part of a broader approach that is underpinned by a recognition of the importance of a long-term and supportive relationship. We will suggest that the relational dynamic and process that were a central part of the early casework approach of social work, is now supported by research from the field of developmental psychology (in particular, studies about attachment), neuroscience and psychotherapy, and that this research also supports the 'conception of relationship, as both a developmental process and as the central organising feature of any treatment endeavour' (Brandell and Ringel 2004). We suggest that the professional-client relationship is a pivotal part of the change process, and that such practice needs to be backed by an organisational structure committed to supporting reflective practice and practitioners.

4.2 How should we be supporting families to change their behaviour?

What we know about what works with complex families

It has been observed that 'practice knowledge now indicates that simply telling people what to do, or how to do it, is rarely effective in supporting people to change their desired behaviors' (Wahab 2005), and that this is particularly true in families experiencing the type of multiple problems with which child abuse is often associated. A recent review of effective practice found no one service approach or method had yet been identified to be effective with complex families where children are at risk of significant harm, and that the effectiveness of manualised programmes has also not been demonstrated (Thoburn 2009). This is an important finding because although there is some evidence highlighting effective, manualised interventions to prevent the occurrence and recurrence of child abuse (eg Hicks and Stein 2010; Montgomery et al.

2009; MacMillan et al. 2009; Barlow et al. 2006), such interventions are likely to represent just one part of the overall package of services required to support families experiencing the sorts of problems referred to above (Thoburn 2009).

So although there are no straightforward answers in terms of 'what works' to support 'multi-problem' and 'resistant' families, evidence concerning the effective implementation of evidence-based and manualised interventions provides important indications about the key elements of practice that are necessary for effective working. For example, Fauth et al. (2010) in a review about effective practice to protect children living with 'resistant' families' point to the need for long-term services rather than episodic interventions, the need to deal openly with the power dynamic between practitioners and family, and to the importance of practitioners conveying empathy and acceptance. However, the authors also suggest that such practices are the necessary but not sufficient condition for success, and that they need to be balanced with an approach that is aimed at containing anxiety and ensuring the child's needs stay in sharp focus. This review also highlights some of the problems associated with working with families in which there is repeated maltreatment or serious injury, including a lack of timely services, the complexities of adults' problems eclipsing the needs of the child, and an inability to identify families who are 'genuinely engaged' in treatment as opposed to those exhibiting 'false compliance', alongside issues such as compromised decision-making and assessment abilities due to a lack of engagement, and hostility on the part of such families.

Consistent with this finding, two further recent reviews also conclude that the over-arching principles for effective help and protection should primarily involve the provision of a dependable professional relationship. Thoburn (2009) examined the effectiveness of interventions for complex families where there are concerns about (or evidence of) a child suffering significant harm, and Barlow and Schrader McMillan (2010) examined interventions where there is evidence of emotional abuse. Both highlight the centrality of the relationship-based intervention, which has at its heart a partnership model of working. Thoburn suggests that particularly in the case of families with whom it is difficult to establish a relationship, the evidence points to the need for experienced practitioners who are highly skilled in terms of relationship-based practice and who have a well-developed capacity for empathising with the family while also retaining in mind the risk of harm to the child. She suggests this also points to the need for highly skilled casework and clinical supervision to provide: a) additional insights and space for reflective functioning; and b) emotional support to social workers who are intervening with such emotionally demanding families.

In summary, there is currently very little evidence to show that discrete, manualised packages can on their own prevent the recurrence of child abuse, and much to suggest that such interventions should be part of a broader approach that involves the provision of a long-term relationship underpinned by some of the theoretical concepts that are now indicated by recent aetiological models of child abuse.

Aetiology of child abuse

In Chapter Two we drew attention to the ecological-transactional framework and to the fact that the research now clearly shows that children's development is significantly shaped by the quality of relationships and interactions with key caretakers across key family domains. Cowan and Cowan (2008) developed a five-domain family process model, which highlights the importance of a number of family relationships in terms of the risk that is presented to children. This model is underpinned by recent research in the field of developmental psychology (Sroufe 1995; 2005) and neuroscience (eg Schore 1994) showing the impact of such relationships on children's social and emotional development. The evidence underpinning the model indicates that attachment relationships are one of the key routes by which intergenerational transmission of relationship patterns takes place, with factors beyond the family creating a range of sources of stress or support (see the ecological-transactional model in Chapter Two and Cowan and Cowan 2008).

In brief, evidence-based aetiological models of abuse suggest that parents who provide parenting that is harmful in terms of their child's development, have mostly been exposed to early environments that did not meet their own developmental needs or that were characterised by trauma.[1] These models suggest that parents who have been exposed to such environments 'find their children's needs and fears overwhelming and profoundly evocative, and as a result often find it difficult to read the most basic cues without distortion or misattribution' (Slade et al. 2005), and consequently respond by withdrawing, or being intrusive and hostile. There is now extensive evidence from attachment and neurological research to show that the early representational and relationship patterns that are developed as a response to such parenting and/or trauma are re-enacted throughout the individual's life, unless the child or parent is provided with the opportunity to revise them as a result of a later relationship[s].

This aetiological model of abuse suggests that abusive parents are in need of an emotionally corrective relationship that consists of two basic features: i) a supportive therapeutic stance based on principles of acceptance, empathy, genuineness and trust, all of which are essential to fostering a strong alliance between client and worker and to meeting some of the parent's unmet developmental needs (eg Luthar et al. 2007), particularly that of containment (discussed later in this chapter); ii) a focus on interpersonal and relational issues with the aim of giving parents an opportunity to reflect on the parenting they are providing in the light of their own experiences of being parented, alongside the opportunity to increase their capacity for some of the aspects of parenting that were highlighted in Box 2.11.

The provision of such relationships is potentially an extremely effective method of working with parents who abuse their children, because in addition to taking account of the systemic factors involved, this approach targets the key developmental processes that are now recognised to have shaped the parent's capacity for emotional regulation, and thereby their capacity for establishing secure, loving and trusting relationships. The evidence suggests that 'assisting people to establish and maintain satisfactory interpersonal relationships' and 'helping them with their emotional difficulties, is the core social work task' (Sudbery 2002), and that such relationship-based working recognises that the 'quality, care and integrity of the worker's response can enable development, maturation and therapeutic progress'. Perhaps most importantly, relationship-based practice draws on two models of psychosocial working - attachment and psychodynamic theory - that are both now underpinned by a strong evidence base and involve an understanding of the individual's real-life experiences. This enables the therapeutic relationship to be used to 'actively engage with the client's real external life - their finance, housing, daily living, their care of children' (Sudbery 2002). Sable (1996) suggests that the application of such an approach provides a 'framework for listening to clients' narratives and putting together a scenario of how their current difficulties originated and developed', alongside the provision of a reparative relationship. This type of working contrasts with the current emphasis on the 'here and now', and the use of brief solution-focused approaches.

1. Research in the field of developmental psychopathology and attachment suggest that many forms of psychopathology should be viewed as forms of adaptation to compromised environments rather than as illness (Page and Norwood 2007).

> **Box 4.1: An attachment framework as the basis for intervention**
>
> 'Together, worker and client re-trace and re-examine clients' attachment-related experiences, noting where responses have been omitted, suppressed or falsified, or where there were injunctions to defensively exclude feelings of attachment. As responses are connected to the events that elicited them, clients begin to understand why they have come to see the world as they do, to reassess their relationships and then to modify their working models.' (Sable 1996)

One of the key theorists working within the field of attachment-based social work practice writes:

> *depending on their analysis of people's attachment behaviours and current social situations, social workers might design their interventions in such a way as to increase clients' exposure to relationships that are secure, responsive, psychologically available, emotionally corrective and positively regarding. The general aim is to increase security, affect regulation and reciprocal adaptation. The social worker herself can provide such a relationship.* (Howe 1998)

The next two sections of the chapter examine: i) the use of evidence-based partnership/ participatory working as the core feature of all intervention strategies, and ii) the use of 'relationship'-based practice, drawing on recent findings about early relational development and the key concepts defining such development (including attachment, rupture and repair, containment, transference and counter-transference, reflective function and projective identification), as an important means of both understanding abusive parenting and as a key mechanism with which to bring about change.

Evidence-based models of partnership working

The Family Partnership Model defines the core stance and process that should be implemented with families by key practitioners working within children's services. This method of working is underpinned by a cognitive, goal-oriented, relational approach to change. It also recognises the significance of the past in terms of current 'constructions' (see below), and can be used alongside the other aspects of relationship-based working, which we examine in the next section. We suggest that a model of this nature should be a core part of the training and practice of professionals in the field of safeguarding because it defines the key processes involved in the helping relationship, alongside the practitioner skills and qualities needed to facilitate this. This represents an approach in which change is facilitated and assessed as part of the process of working in partnership through the negotiation of short-term goals, which parents are then helped to achieve. The use of such an approach can provide some indication of parental capacity for change, in addition to addressing issues such as 'false compliance' (Crispin Day, personal communication; Harnett and Day 2008).

The Family Partnership Model, which teaches practitioners the core components of the helping relationship, is one of the best available evidence-based participatory models of working with families. It requires that practitioners are trained in its principles and implementation, and receive ongoing support in its application. It is based on the 'constructionist' work of Kelly (1991), which defines 'how people function psychologically and socially' and suggests that 'both parents and helpers develop a unique understanding of their world in order to anticipate and adapt to events'. A major implication of this is that the process of facilitating change involves 'challenging parental constructions' to enable parents to develop more useful or effective constructions (see Box 4.2). For a full description of the model, see Davis, Day and Bidmead (2002), Braun, Davis and Mansfield (2006) and Davis and Day (2010).

> Box 4.2: Construing - a model of how people construct understanding of their world
>
> > all people construct a model of the world in their head
>
> > the model derives from experience
>
> > the model enables anticipation and determines action
>
> > each person is unique
>
> > constructions may not be conscious or verbalised
>
> > constructions evolve over time
>
> > social interaction is determined by our constructions of each other's constructions

Davis (2009) suggests that:

> since the task of building a relationship between the helper and the parent is crucial to the facilitation of the whole [helping] process and hence the outcomes, the nature of the relationship to which health professionals should work must be carefully defined and represented as a specific ingredient within the overall model.

Perhaps most importantly, Davis suggests that effective partnership working is characterised by: i) working closely together with active participation and involvement; ii) sharing decision-making power; iii) recognition of complementary expertise and roles; iv) sharing and agreeing aims and the process for how to achieve them; v) negotiation of disagreement; vi) mutual trust and respect, and openness and honesty; and vii) clear communication.

The Family Partnership Model defines the core tasks of the helping process (see Figure 4.1), and also defines the core 'internal qualities' required by practitioners in order to work effectively in partnership. These include respect, genuineness, empathy, humility, quiet enthusiasm, personal integrity, attunement and technical knowledge (including an understanding of the helping process).

Figure 4.1: The process of helping: tasks

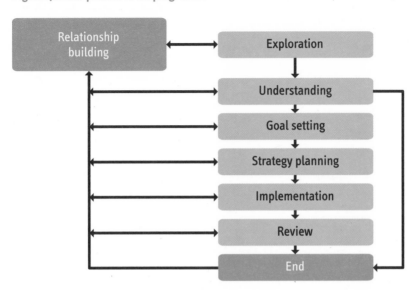

Interventions underpinned by cognitive-behavioural models of change are possibly one of the most widely evidence-based models of intervention now available, and Motivational Interviewing provides a further example of a cognitively-based method of partnership-working with families to bring about change. Wahab (2005) describes it as 'an exciting intervention model for numerous social work settings due to its consistency with core social work values, ethics, resources, and evidence-based practice'. It is underpinned by the Transtheoretical Model (Prochaska and DiClemente 1982), and is informed by seven distinct theories: conflict and ambivalence; decisional balance; health beliefs; reactance; self-perception theory; self-regulation theory; and value theory. Like the Family Partnership Model, Motivational Interviewing has at its heart the importance of establishing a relationship of trust, and of 'acceptance' and 'unconditional positive regard' (Rogers 1957; 1959 cited in Wahab 2005).

Motivational Interviewing conceptualises behaviour change as comprising a number of stages along a continuum of 'motivational readiness' that includes pre-contemplation, contemplation, preparation, action, maintenance and relapse. The overall aim 'is to support people to move along a continuum of behaviour change by creating a supportive, non-judgemental, directive environment to facilitate the exploration of one's motivations, readiness and confidence levels for change as well as ambivalence to change' (Wahab 2005).

As with the Family Partnership Model discussed above, the spirit of Motivational Interviewing involves the 'intention and the gestalt of the practitioner's disposition with the client', which 'transcends the mechanisms of the practice by supporting and providing the foundation for the skills and techniques' (Wahab 2005). This 'availability and willingness to be present enough with a client to glimpse their inner world' through the implementation of empathic and reflective listening is used in the implementation of Motivational Interviewing skills and techniques, the four basic principles of which are: expressing; developing discrepancy; rolling with resistance; and supporting self-efficacy (Wahab 2005).

Motivational Interviewing also teaches practitioners about the helping process and requires that they are trained in its principles and implementation, and receive ongoing support in its application. It is underpinned by extensive evidence regarding its

effectiveness in working with individuals and families to bring about change
(see Wahab 2005 for an overview of the evidence about Motivational Interviewing,
and Davis 2009 for an overview of the evidence about the effectiveness of the Family
Partnership Model).

The next section examines the key aspects of 'relationship-based' practice,
which it will be suggested should be core to all safeguarding work.

Relationship-based practice - what should be involved?

Alongside the use of cognitively-based partnership models of working, the research also
suggests the importance of what we are defining as 'relationship-based' practice, in terms
of bringing about change with complex families in which child protection is of concern.
In Chapter Two we discussed the findings from research about infant development and
its relational context. We suggested that this emerging body of research strongly indicates
that the core needs of an infant (ie for a parent who is capable of attunement and repair
to ruptures, containment, and reflective functioning) are, in fact, also key to understanding
what should be provided as part of effective relationship-based practice. We will suggest
here that other concepts derived from psychoanalytic theory (including transference/
counter-transference and projective identification) provide significant tools for social
workers both to understand the behaviour of complex families and help them to change.
Indeed, such concepts are fundamental to an understanding of the 'inherently complex
psycho-social processes' (Walker 2008) at work in families in which abuse is occurring.
They are also necessary to address the strategies that social workers use 'to defend
against witnessing emotional pain and suffering in others' (Walker 2008) and to protect
against the emergence of organisational structures (of which managerialism and
proceduralism are prime examples) that are developed to defend against such anxiety
(Menzies-Lyth 1960).

Although some of what follows may feel to experienced social workers like coming
full circle, there is now a strong evidence base to underpin such practice. Perhaps most
interestingly, some of the key concepts that we will suggest are core to such practice
derive from the fields of infant mental health, attachment and psychotherapeutic theory.
Alongside what is known about 'what works' from evidence-based models of intervention
such as the Family Nurse Partnership programme (Rowe 2009), these findings in relation
to infant development indicate the key factors necessary for successful therapeutic work.

Recognising the past in the present

In Chapter Two we examined recent evidence about the core developmental processes in
infancy, and, in particular, attachment theory, which has demonstrated quite clearly the
way in which early experiences with caretakers are internalised in the form of 'internal
working models'. These then inform the way an individual feels about him/herself and
their relations with other people. Such working models play a significant role in the
infant/toddler's evolving sense of self and their capacity for later relationships. For
example, it was suggested that 'disorganised attachment' is a frequent outcome of
neglectful, abusive or traumatic parenting in the early years, leading to a range of later
developmental and psychological problems. Perhaps most importantly, such patterns of
relating are established early in life and occur at an unconscious level. Indeed, it is the
unconscious nature of these patterns that contributes to them being re-enacted in later
relationships, including relationships with children. Box 4.3 provides two examples of
the significant ways in which interactions with children in the present can evoke painful
childhood memories that then become the basis for future abusive parenting.

> **Box 4.3: Clinical vignettes**
>
> 'a) Mary is angry, demands a lot of attention from the therapists and ignores her baby. The therapists try to calm her down and ask her to tell them what has happened. She describes how her baby's fingers had clung to her hair at home, and how it caused a strong reaction in her: "I lost my temper and I remembered how my mother dragged me by the hair with my feet 10cm from the ground. I left the baby crying and I went to the balcony for a cigarette to calm my nerves..."
>
> b) Linda always feeds her baby with unheated milk. During lunch we discuss the memories that the mothers have of food when they were little children. Linda finds a connection between the cold bottle and her childhood experience. She remembers how her own mother and baby-sitter forced her to eat and drink food and liquids so hot that her mouth was burned over and over again.' (Belt and Punamaki 2007)

The two clinical examples in Box 4.3 are taken from a group-based parent-infant psychotherapy programme, one of many such interventions now being developed (see Barlow and Schrader McMillan 2010 for further discussion) that aim to help parents understand their current parenting practices and ways of relating, in the light of past experiences. They are aimed at helping parents to experience the past in the context of a present, containing relationship with both the therapist and the group, and also to think about, understand and contain the very powerful feelings that can be evoked by a child. This is demonstrated by the following example:

> *Julia is a four-month-old baby girl, whose mother Ann is neglecting her needs. Even in the winter in the freezing cold, Ann dresses Julia lightly and gives her too little milk from a dirty feeding bottle. Ann is always very hungry and greedily eats the food that is served in the group. In the first sessions the therapists allow her to concentrate on her own needs, but gradually they and group members express their worry about the adequacy of Julia's feeding and the warmth of her clothing. The therapists make a whole-group interpretation of the mother-infant ravenous hunger and unsatisfied need, and how Ann very clearly expresses group members' hunger for the group's care. Other members of the group have already discreetly taken responsibility for the situation. In the following session one of the mothers brings her own baby's nice warm clothes for Ann, who proudly puts them on Julia. The other mothers show how they prepare milk and gauge their babies' hunger. Ann feels that the group has understood her and appreciates her, and she accepts the advice. She soon dresses Julia warmly, gives her more food and holds her more closely. Gradually, Julia's weight increases, and her interaction with Ann becomes more active, to the extent that Ann complains that she gets tired of Julia's liveliness.* (Belt and Punamaki 2007)

This type of working involves taking account of the 'transference', which refers to 'the process of a person re-creating her or his patterns of emotional experience in the context of the present therapeutic relationship' (Flaskas 2007). Flaskas has written widely about the way in which an understanding of what is happening in terms of the transference between client and worker not only enables 'empathic connection' but also enables the worker to use 'difficulties in therapeutic engagement and impasse to further, rather than hinder, the therapeutic process' (Flaskas 2007).

For example, a parent who abuses their child will often have experienced early parenting that is inconsistent, neglectful or abusive. They will have developed one of a limited number of potential internal working models of self, and self in relation to others, which it would have been possible to identify when they were children, and which has continued with them into adult life and relationships. For example, a majority of maltreated children are classified as being disorganised or disorientated in their attachment behaviour.[4] These children attempt to solve the 'irresolvable paradox' of their parents' behaviour by trying to meet their parents' attachment needs, and thereby retaining 'a level of safe proximity and involvement' (Howe 2005; Howe et al. 1999). Typical patterns of behaviour shown by such children include 'controlling' behaviours that involve 'compulsive compliance' in which the child becomes highly submissive; 'compulsive caregiving' in which the child parents the parent; and an 'aggressive-fearful' pattern characterised by a range of highly antisocial and maladaptive behaviours (see, for example, Box 4.4).

> **Box 4.4: Compulsive caregiving**
>
> 'Caroline is 18 months old. She lives with her mother, who is chronically depressed. The mother describes the household as 'noxious to the soul'. She cannot tolerate the idea that her depression is affecting Caroline. She says: "Caroline is the only one who makes me laugh." It is observed that Caroline silently enacts the role of a clown. She disappears into her room and comes out wearing increasingly more preposterous costumes. Caroline makes her mother laugh, but she herself never laughs... As this pattern becomes better established, it further consolidates the child's maladaptive perceptions of self, others and emotional relationships.' (Howe et al. 1999)

Such relationship patterns are continued into adulthood where they are often re-enacted in the parent-child relationship, and also in the relationship with the social worker. However, it is only possible to understand such functioning in the present if social workers are able to spend time with clients exploring the past. The 'transference' could therefore be used by social workers to develop a better understanding of the early relationship patterns of a particular client and thereby to understand their existing patterns of relating, including those with their children. This involves social workers having the skills and training to enable them to recognise that parents who abuse their children are re-enacting in the present aspects of their own traumatic past.

The 'counter-transference' can similarly be used to help social workers understand such relationship patterns and develop different methods of relating. The counter-transference refers to 'the emotions, attitudes and patterns of relating which the therapist may begin to experience and enact in the context of the therapeutic relationship' (Flaskas 2007). Such counter-transference reactions can be a result of both the therapist's own transferences or 'a more complex interaction of the therapist's unconscious processes and the clients' ways of relating'. Either way, the social worker needs both to have developed some awareness of their own patterns of relating and to have the necessary space, as part of a supervisory process, to reflect on counter-transference feelings, and the ways in which they may help or hinder the therapeutic process.

The concept of 'projective identification' is also potentially useful to effective working with parents experiencing complex problems. Flaskas (2007) suggests this concept 'bridges both the unconscious experience of the client/s, and the connection and

---

4. This occurs as a result of parenting in which the carer's own attachment needs are dominant or in which the parent is either frightened or frightening.

potential of the therapeutic relationship'. It refers to an 'intensely relational process, for it describes not just the momentum of a person to split off and unconsciously project unbearable impasses of emotion and meaning, but also the way in which these impasses come to be communicated in the context of a relationship'. Box 4.5 provides an example of the way in which such projective identification can be observed in a parent who is 'unable to tolerate his or her own emotional experience in relation to the child' and in which the child serves as a repository of unbearable feelings from the parent. Lieberman (1999) suggests that such processes involve the emotional abuse of a child, and are the basis of later domestic violence.

Box 4.5: Projective identification in practice

Shirley, who has witnessed her father regularly beat her mother and was physically abused by her father, is now in a relationship with a man in which domestic violence is a strong feature. Shirley has a three-year-old son Jason, to whom she attributes some of the violent impulses that characterise her experience of men, thereby distorting normal angry behaviour and treating it as evidence that he has an aggressive personality.

Shirley also exerts direct pressure on her son to conform to these attributions by dressing him in a leather jacket, calling him names such as 'vicious', 'monster', 'devil' and 'evil', and by ignoring or ridiculing his signals of anxiety and vulnerability by telling him that he is being manipulative, and by being rough and bossy with him. When Jason responds with anger, Shirley is at a loss to know how to manage his behaviour effectively, which escalates into increasingly more coercive and violent exchanges. (adapted from Lieberman 1999)

This research points to the importance of understanding these processes in terms of how they are enacted in the client-worker relationship, and their role in communicating client needs and level of functioning, which is essential to enabling change.

Further findings from infant research

In discussing the underpinning concepts in Chapter Two, we referred to findings from infant research that point to the importance for infant development of a parent who is able to be attuned and to repair ruptures, to contain the infant's overwhelming anxiety, and to see the infant or child as an 'intentional being' thereby providing what has been called 'reflective function'. This section will examine the importance of these concepts in terms of the type of relationship-based working needed between social worker and client in order to enable change to occur, and also in terms of the way in which such skills are key to successful interprofessional communication, and broader organisational functioning (see for example Howe submitted).

Psychoanalytic theory and research in the field of infant mental health have pointed to two key phases of infant development. The first takes place during the first three months of life prior to the development of the capacity for symbolisation or psychic structure, and is referred to as 'paranoid-schizoid' because it is characterised by the infant's need to manage intolerable anxiety by attempting to get rid of it onto an external object through a process that is known as 'projective identification' (discussed above). This process of 'projective identification' is viewed as being a normal process and it is now thought that infants need to organise their 'chaotic experience by splitting and projecting good and bad feelings resulting in a severance of love or hate'. Furthermore, 'this phase is dominated by confusion between self and object, by concrete thinking and by rigid defences characteristic of psychosis' (Mandin 2007).

While the paranoid-schizoid position involves the rigid use of defences against anxiety, the next phase of development, called the 'depressive position', involves greater integration because:

> [the] infant starts to recognise whole objects, to remember and to anticipate. S/he realises that good and bad objects may be part of the same person or object and therefore has to learn to tolerate that experiences such as love and hate do co-exist side by side. During the depressive position the infant has to face up to a number of painful realisations in order to achieve the healthy integration described by Bion (1967) and develop a reparative capacity. (Mandin 2007)

The process of 'maternal containment' is now thought to be key to the process by which infants navigate the early movement between the above two strategies, and thereby to their increasing capacity for affect regulation, and to their developing capacity for linking, symbolisation and thought. Flaskas (2007) suggests that Bion's theories about containment:

> offer one of the most intensely relational understandings of the development of the capacity to think (see Bion 1967; 1970), arguing that the conditions for the development of this capacity occur in pre-verbal relationships in which we are being thought about and held in mind (and body) by another. The containment offered by another who is trying to know us and think about our experience thus becomes the relational condition of our capacity to know ourselves.

Toasland (2007) refers to Bion's (1967) description of the way in which mothers who are in a suitable frame of mind (referred to as 'reverie') are able to accept the powerful feelings that are raised by the infant's expression of emotions, to process them and, through touch, gesture or speech, to give them back to the infant in a more manageable form. The parallel between the mother and her baby, and that of the practitioner and client, is now thought to be an important one in terms of the processes taking place. It is suggested that 'by recognising and experiencing the client's unbearable feelings, the worker helps the client to develop an internal container for their distressing feelings' (Toasland 2007). This is particularly important because there is increasing consensus that parents who abuse their children have experienced significant failure in their early environment, and that this has left them without an internalised container for their painful feelings of anger and shame, which are consequently enacted with their children, thereby repeating the cycle of violence. Evidence from the field of psychotherapy suggests that a long-term containing, 'therapeutic' relationship can help such individuals to begin to change the ways in which they relate.

Box 4.6 Containment

'During these early phases of development, the infant is thought to be particularly dependent on the primary carer's capacity to hold the baby's primitive anxieties which can be projected onto her in order to relieve him from pain. This requires the carer to stay attuned in order to give back to the baby the baby's own self. It involves an active process called 'containment' in which key carers are able to use their mind to be receptive to the infant's need to project unbearable anxieties into her and through the use of touch, gesture, speech etc. to make such anxiety containable thereby allowing the infant to introject a maternal container as a result of the parent's containment of their distressing feelings: an internal object to enable them to manage these feelings more effectively in the future.' (Toasland 2007)

The concept of containment should be used as a significant part of a relationship-based approach, not only to understand the violent feelings that are sometimes expressed by such clients (ie in terms of early environmental failure to provide them with a means of containing such feelings), but also in terms of the need for individuals working within safeguarding to provide the type of relationship that can enable the client to begin to internalise a container (ie a corrective emotional experience) and to meet some of the client's unmet dependency needs.

Concepts such as containment are also important at an organisational level, and there is increasing recognition of the need for 'containment of the container' (Toasland 2007). In other words, professionals (who are containing the overwhelming feelings of clients) need managers and supervisors who are able to receive the projections of the practitioners and to process them in order to make them manageable, thereby providing some containment for staff. Toasland (2007) refers to the work of Bion who distinguishes between three types of container-contained relations. The first is 'parasitic', in which there is an unhealthy and destructive dependence upon the manager or supervisor as a result of the latter being able to receive the worker's projections but unable to 'effectively re-project these into the worker to enable them to develop their internal container'. In such circumstances, projections remain with the manager 'in a passive, holding capacity and create a dependent relationship with the worker'. The second type, which is defined as being 'symbiotic', is one in which the worker depends on the manager or supervisor for support, 'while receiving the manager's re-projections in order to strengthen his internal container' and to help him/her manage the many very difficult feelings that are inevitably raised by this type of work. Bion's third type is a commensal relationship, which could be equated with a peer supervision relationship 'with both parties benefiting from mutual containment' (see Box 4.7).

Box 4.7: Containment in practice

'A practitioner in my team undertook a piece of therapeutic work with a 17-year-old young woman who was self-harming and displaying obsessional behavior. This young woman had a history of sexual abuse and trauma which she found difficult to verbalise. The work used a variety of creative techniques to help her to explore her feelings. The pattern of sessions with this young woman was characterised by repeated missed sessions, particularly after breaks. The therapeutic worker would finish sessions exhausted and frustrated, sometimes complaining of severe headaches. Supervision of this case explored both the unconscious processes in the relationship between the practitioner and the client, and acknowledged and worked through the worker's frustrations and feelings of being worn down and incapable in response to this young woman. I was fortunate in managing a worker who was able to articulate her feelings and was reflective about the nature of the work. However, I was required to experience this frustration and helplessness myself in order to assist her in making this manageable. Together we explored the dynamics underlying the relationship between practitioner and client, and acknowledged the impact of the young woman's projections. In particular, the practitioner explicitly commented on her headaches, and these subsequently ceased once the feelings underlying them were made conscious.' (Boyd 2007)

It has been recognised over recent years that social care agencies have

> *struggled to manage an excess of anxiety at the coal face of the work, leading to changes within social work culture, with the organisation less effectively managing this anxiety and increasingly expecting workers to manage it themselves... [As a result, there is] a sense of continually changing boundaries with no stable system to protect and contain workers, who are engaged in complex relationships with service users and colleagues.* (Toasland 2007)

The consequence of a manager whose containment is not good enough are a reduction in the practitioner's capacity to work effectively with clients, and for the worker then to feel overwhelmed with unprocessed anxiety and eventually to leave the job. This is currently expressed very clearly in the rapid turn-over of staff in social care.

In Chapter Two we examined the nature of the 'proto-conversational' turn-taking, which takes place between an infant and her attuned care-taker, and the periods of disruption following periods of synchrony, which skilled caretakers are able to 'repair'. Many abusive parents will have received early care-taking in which there was either no attunement or no repair to these ruptures, resulting in them experiencing 'powerful feelings of anger, fear or shame when disruption occurs' (Walker 2008). The ruptures that inevitably happen as a result of the relationship with the social worker will result in feelings of anger and shame on the part of the client, leading to withdrawal or attack. This points to the importance of practitioners being aware that many parents with whom they work will be 'vulnerable to being misunderstood and not listened to as a result of their very early experiences' (Walker 2008). They also need to be aware of the potential impact that inevitable ruptures to communication (ie in which the emotional synchrony between them is lost) will have on the client, and of the need to work hard to repair them. Indeed, a central part of relationship-based work with such clients should involve increasing the capacity of the client to manage such ruptures, which are an inevitable part of all relationships. This requires the provision of a long-term relationship in which the client can gradually come to see that repair to ruptures is possible.

The need for social workers to manage such ruptures when they occur as part of interprofessional communication is also increasingly recognised. Walker (2008) provides an example in which a social worker, experiencing a moment of rupture or potential conflict in relation to discussions with a doctor, may quickly re-experience feelings of shame or of not being 'good enough'. He goes on to suggest that:

> *when faced with such feelings, one response would be for the social worker to withdraw out of a sense of shame and not pursue her argument ... The social worker may lack sufficient resilience to be able to tolerate this moment of disruption without being transported back to earlier, traumatic experiences of disruption.*

Such feelings may also reflect feelings of inadequacy and helplessness on the part of the doctor being projected into the social worker. Walker goes on to suggest that 'child protection work can evoke very powerful, primitive feelings in us, which touch us and our relationships with our primary carers on a deep level. Faced with such stresses the likelihood is that we will fall back on earlier modes of functioning.' It has been suggested that a major consequence of this failure to repair ruptures to communication is the type of mis-communication that has been such a dominant feature of many child protection inquiries (see Walker 2008 for an overview).

Safeguarding professionals, and social workers in particular, will be repeatedly exposed to the experience of ruptures, and to projections from other colleagues that leave them feeling angry, distressed and full of shame, and there is a need to allow workers to talk about and work through such experiences in order to enable them to 'continue to work creatively and openly' (Walker 2008). This requires the development of an organisational culture in which 'vulnerability can be acknowledged and shared', (Walker 2008) and recognition that the absence of de-briefings or opportunities to reflect on these events is a significant cause of burn-out throughout the profession.[5]

The third concept that is repeatedly highlighted across the literature in terms of its potential importance for increasing the capacity of social workers for relationship-based work, is that of 'reflective function' (Walker 2008), which was described more fully in Chapter Two. It is now thought that an inability for 'reflective function' is a central part of the pathology of individuals with personality disorders (Fonagy et al. 2003), and that a key part of therapeutic work should involve attempts to increase reflective function in clients, particularly in the field of child protection. Walker (2008) provides an example of a 13-year-old girl who had become increasingly aggressive and critical towards her mother. He suggests that the girl's mother lacked a capacity for reflective function because she was unable to think about possible explanations for such behaviour. The mother 'could only understand her [daughter's] behaviour in terms of how she experienced it, ie as vicious attacks on her'. This example demonstrates the way in which such parents may be unable, without a skilled therapeutic relationship-based intervention, to recognise that the behaviour of children may occur for a range of reasons. This phenomenon can often be seen in parents of very young children who attribute intent to a young child's crying (ie to get at them), which is developmentally beyond the infant's capacity. A lack of capacity for such reflective functioning puts a child at increased risk of abuse. Box 4.8 provides a further description of reflective function.

> ### Box 4.8: Reflective function
>
> 'It is suggested that a well-developed capacity for reflective functioning or mentalisation is what enables the person to distinguish inner reality from outer reality, pretend modes from 'real' modes of functioning. From this perspective, disturbed and abusive parents obliterate their children's affective experience - emotions that are not held in mind by the caregiver, or, more significantly, that are misrepresented or distorted, remain diffuse, terrifying and unrepresentable to the child. This may give rise to a range of borderline phenomena and pathology of the self in later years.' (Renn 2009)

Walker (2008) suggests relationship-based work should involve the use of questions such as: 'Why do you think you behaved in this way?', 'Why do you think your partner was violent to you?' and 'Why do you think your social worker is worried about you?', in order to invite clients to 'explore the possible meaning of another person's behaviour'. The responses to such questions are important because 'a parent who is able to recognise that a child is crying because she is upset, hungry or frightened is more likely to respond benignly than one who is feeling that the child's crying is intentional and that she is persecuting or attacking them'. Walker goes on to suggest that assessing reflective function enables social workers to both make a more accurate assessment of risk and to better understand 'an individual's potential vulnerability in terms of their capacity to communicate and relate'. Bateman and Fonagy (2004) describe the use of such an approach to promote change in individuals with borderline personality disorder.

---

5. The need for supervision to fulfill such a role raises questions as to whether this can be adequately provided for where the supervisor is also the case manager.

A capacity for reflective functioning is also crucial in terms of effective interprofessional and interagency communication. Walker (2008) cites an example provided by Fonagy (1999) which suggests that the absence of reflective practice results in a stereotyping of other professional groups thereby rendering them inhuman, whereas reflective practice provides the opportunity to reflect on the fact that other people may have a different perspective or that one's own understanding may be restricted. An analysis of Part 8 Reviews in Wales found that communication failures in the field of child protection often originated from 'a lack of respect or mistrust of other professionals' perspectives' (Walker 2008).

Box 4.9: Working to improve reflective function

Mia, who lived with her boyfriend Jay in his parents' chaotic and dirty house, was doing everything she could to disavow the reality of the baby and of her own internal world and referred to the infant as 'that' or 'my belly'. This unwanted pregnancy interfered with Mia's own desire, and her mother's hope that Mia would get an education. Mia had a remarkable ability to verbalise her feelings of pain, anxiety and confusion about the child, something which was a valuable resource to the intervention team. The two practitioners began by helping Mia 'make room' for her child by creating a physical space for the baby and helping her envision and plan for an infant's physical needs.

Mia gave birth to a healthy girl but suffered from post-partum depression which peaked a month after birth. Mia rejected psychiatric treatment, and it was agreed that in addition to nursing visits, a social worker would visit her weekly. Mia cared for Noni physically but did not willingly touch her and left her alone for extended periods. At this point it was possible to start discussing Mia's past, and over the next few months, Mia forged a relationship with the social worker, in which she allowed herself to remember and describe moments and fears long forgotten, creating a narrative about her past that enabled her to better understand the present.

Mia sometimes engaged in threatening behaviours, looming over the child, apparently delighting in the infant's grimace and frozen expression and asserting that the infant was 'faking' hunger cues. Workers did not address these deficits directly, but instead helped Mia to understand the emotion that the baby's crying elicited and to trace a causal link between events in her past and her reaction to the child. As the intervention proceeded, Mia began to view the baby's intentions and affects with increasing accuracy and clarity, without needing to distort them in order to protect her fragile sense of self. Slowly, she became able to step outside her automatic reactions and observe her child's feelings. The baby began to express a more extended range of emotions to her now available mother.

When Noni was 14 months old (17 months after Mia had entered the programme) the social worker reviewed a videotape made when the baby was 4 months old. Mia was troubled by her own lack of sensitivity, noting signs of distress that she was now able to identify. At 20 months, the baby was thriving, showed signs of secure attachment and was clearly loved by her mother, father (who still lived with his own family but was involved with his daughter) and her extended family. (Slade et al. 2005)

In summary, we have pointed to the importance of relationship-based working that is not only underpinned by systemic practices, but also by learning from both attachment and psychoanalytic theory (ie including concepts regarding the transference/counter-transference, containment, and projective identification for example), in addition to findings from infant mental health (ie regarding rupture and repair in communications, and other concepts such as reflective function). We have sought to indicate the importance of such working not only in terms of addressing some of the unmet developmental needs of clients who may be behaving abusively towards their children, but also in terms of the needs of social workers for effective communication with other professionals, and for containment by the sort of organisational structures that offer the necessary opportunities for reflective exchanges, and that thereby function as a 'secure base' (Walker 2008).

4.3 Evidence-based methods of changing parenting capacity and the parent-child relationship

In addition to partnership and relationship-based practice, intervention with families in which there is concern that a parent may be abusing a child should be goal-focused and explicitly aim to bring about change in parenting capacity and the parent-child relationship through the application of evidence-based interventions. Evidence about working effectively to bring about such change varies according to the age of the child, and this section therefore comprises two parts. The first addresses working with families in which the child is less than four years of age, and the second addresses working with parents of children five years or above.

Where there is concern about a parent harming a child, the evidence suggests that the following three steps should be taken, in the context of the partnership and relationship-based practice (discussed above), for children of all ages.

1. An early assessment should be made of parenting capacity, parent-infant/child interaction, and parental readiness and capacity for change. This should include the use of standardised instruments to appraise some of the key parenting tasks that have been referred to above, as part of a structured clinical assessment (see Chapter Three).

2. A number of evidence-based methods of improving parenting have been identified, but many of these require specialist skills (see below for further details). A Team Around the Child model should be utilised to ensure that such specialist provision is in place.

3. All intervention should be accompanied by an assessment of the extent to which such change has occurred.

In the rest of this section we summarise the evidence about what works to improve parenting where child abuse of an infant or toddler is of concern, and where abuse of older children is a concern. We then examine what a Team Around the Child model involves demonstrating the consistency of this model of working with broader policy changes particularly in terms of the CAF, and conclude by suggesting the importance of assessing the parent's capacity to change, within the context of the services being provided, in order to make important decisions about the need to remove the child from the parental home.

Working effectively to change early parenting

We have argued throughout this document that the first few years of a child's life are fundamental to their capacity for adaption throughout the remainder of their life. The most important aspect of the early environment is the child's relationship with their key caretakers because of its impact on their capacity to regulate their emotions via a secure attachment relationship, and thereby its impact on the child's rapidly developing brain. There is currently a need for considerable improvement in terms of the identification and treatment of neglect and abuse during the first three years of life. More effective practice during this period could not only prevent many of the deaths that currently occur at this age, but could also prevent much of the harm that is done in terms of children's development during this important period.

The evidence suggests that intervention during the first four years needs to be provided as soon as possible, and ideally to be focused on working dyadically with the parent and infant, or parent and child. Over the past two decades a number of such attachment-based interventions have been developed to improve 'the sensitivity and responsiveness of parental behavior in the context of interaction with the child' (Tarabulsy et al. 2008), thereby reducing the likelihood of insecure or disorganised attachment. For example, a recent review demonstrated the effectiveness of a range of interventions to improve parental sensitivity (ie predictability, coherence, warmth etc) and attachment security (Bakermans-Kranenburg et al. 2003). However, only some of these interventions have been shown to be effective with parents at the more severe end of the spectrum (see for example, Barlow and Schrader McMillan 2010). This reflects the severity of the problems in parents who abuse their children, including their lack of ability for attunement, containment and/or reflective function, which frequently occur in the context of parental mental health problems, drug misuse, domestic violence or a history of abuse, being 'in care' or unresolved trauma.

Some of the strongest evidence of effectiveness with such families comes from studies of parent-infant psychotherapy, which focuses on both 'representations' and 'interactions'. Parent-infant psychotherapy uses current interaction between parent and child to gain an understanding of 'the influences of maternal representation on parenting as maternal representations and distortions are enacted within the context of preschooler-parent interactions' (Toth et al. 2002). The therapy is used to explore the parent's history and to promote understanding of the links between this and their current parenting, within the context of a corrective emotional experience between parent and therapist (see Box 4.10). This particular approach focuses on the mother's 'representational' world or the way in which the mother's current view of her child is affected by interfering representations from her own history. The aim of such interventions is to help the mother to recognise the 'ghosts in the nursery' and to link them to her own past and current history, thereby facilitating new paths for growth and development for both mother and infant (Cramer and Stern 1988; see Box 4.11).

Box 4.10: Parent-infant psychotherapy

'Maltreating mothers, who often have childhood histories of disturbed parent-child relationships and frequent negative experiences with social services systems, often expect rejection, abandonment, criticism and ridicule. Through empathy, respect, concern, and unfailing positive regard, therapists help maltreating mothers to overcome these negative expectations and provide a holding environment for the mother and pre-schooler in which new experiences of self in relationship to others and to the pre-schooler may be internalised.' (Toth et al. 2002)

Box 4.11: Psychotherapy and interaction guidance

This case study involves 'S', a one-month-old first-born child of two young parents referred by the community health nurse because of concerns about the mother's possible post-natal depression. At the first home visit, therapists observed the infant's feeding difficulties (although 'S' had not reached the failure to thrive threshold) and noted the negative attributions of the mother ('A') of her baby's behaviour. 'A' said, for example, that the infant 'is angry at me all the time, even when I feed her'.

'A' had a history of severe deprivation as the child of a drug-dependent mother, and had been sexually and emotionally abused. One particular traumatic loss appeared to influence 'A's feelings towards 'S'. 'A' had witnessed the death of her nine-year-old sister in an accident. 'A's loss was projected onto the child. She was filled with remorse at not having saved her sister's life, while at the same time believing that in some way, her sister had been reborn as 'S'. The child's cries represented her (dead) sister's anger.

Therapists had three objectives: (i) to help 'A' differentiate between her dead sister and the child; (ii) to provide developmental guidance; and (iii) to help create an emotional space for the child's true self, rather than the child imagined by her parent, by voicing the child's needs.

Two treatment modalities were combined: mother-infant psychodynamic therapy and interactional guidance, which is explicitly based on strengths. Practitioners try to convey that parents are doing the best they can, address what parents see as the problem, answer questions posed by the family, provide information when asked and jointly with parents define treatment goals and success.

The treatment stages focused on: (i) provision of nurture for 'A', in order to help her become able to care for the child; (ii) enabling 'A' to create a symbolic representation of the child (for example, the therapist sometimes spoke in lieu of the child, 'voicing' the child's feelings and desires); (iii) helping A to mourn her sister's death when S's cognitive and motor skills developed and it became clear to 'A' that 'S' was not her dead sister.

Therapy ended when 'S' was 18 months old, but resumed after 'S' developed selective mutism after starting school. At this point the father, who had resisted treatment, became involved, enabling some resolution of partner conflict. Dyadic therapy ended when the child was four, but both mother and child were referred to individual treatment. (Keren, Feldman and Tyano 2001)

More recently behavioural approaches have been introduced within parent-infant/toddler psychotherapy (Cohen et al. 1999). For example, Watch, Wait and Wonder is an infant/toddler-led parent-infant psychotherapy which involves the mother spending time observing her child's self-initiated activity, accepting their spontaneous and undirected behaviour, and being physically accessible to the child. The mother then discusses her experiences of the play with the therapist with a view to examining the mother's internal working models of herself in relation to her child. There is a growing body of evidence pointing to the effectiveness of parent-infant/toddler psychotherapy (Cohen et al. 2002).

Many of these innovative methods of working during the first four years of life require specialist training. This requires that parent-infant/child psychotherapists are core members of the multidisciplinary Team Around the Child (see below).

Working effectively to change later parenting

Intervention with families in which an older child is at risk should also involve the use of standardised assessment and focus on improving both parenting capacity and the parent-child relationship. The evidence points to the importance of increasing the capacity of parents for warm and affectively sensitive caretaking that facilitates the child's feelings of safety, and their capacity for secure attachment relationships, alongside the use of more positive methods of discipline and supervision.

The research suggests that the use of positive methods of parenting is likely to improve the parent-child relationship and thereby the child's emotional and behavioural functioning, and a number of systematic reviews have highlighted the benefits of manualised programmes for specific groups of abusive parents (eg physically abusive parents - Montgomery et al 2009; emotionally abusive parents - Barlow and Schrader McMillan 2010; neglect - Hicks and Stein 2010). Thoburn (2009) suggests, however, that these are most usefully applied in the UK to families with complex needs as 'one of a range of centre-based services or alongside social casework and other Team Around the Child services (see for example Tunstill et al 2009)'. She goes on to suggest that such parent-focused interventions are most promising where they are based on clear models geared to strengthening the parent-child interactions and reducing child conduct problems (Thoburn 2009).

One example of such a programme is Parents Under Pressure, which is a newly developed intervention underpinned by an ecological model of child development that targets multiple domains of family functioning, including the psychological functioning of individuals in the family, parent-child relationships, and social contextual factors. Perhaps most uniquely, the programme incorporates 'mindfulness' skills that are aimed at improving parental affect regulation. Parents Under Pressure comprises an intensive, manualised, home-based intervention of ten modules conducted in the family home over 10 to 12 weeks, each lasting between one and two hours. The first two modules involve a comprehensive family assessment and individual case formulation, which is conducted collaboratively with the family, and targets for change are identified. Box 4.12 describes the content of modules 3 to 10.

The limited evidence that is available suggests the benefits of standardised programmes of this nature (see for example Harnett and Dawe 2008) particularly where they incorporate additional components that explicitly target aspects of parental functioning that are often compromised in complex families, such as stress management, problem-solving and anger management, and attributional retraining (eg Sanders et al. 2004). The evidence suggests, for example, that 'an intervention aimed at developing a parent's repertoire of parenting skills will have a greater impact on family functioning if the intervention also provides parents with skills to regulate their emotional state, deal more effectively with competing demands, and engage social support' (Harnett and Dawe 2008). Recent evidence suggests that even the use of an intensive evidence-based programme, such as the one described above, will require additional ongoing support to enable parents both to reach a minimal level of adequate parenting, and then maintain it (Harnett and Dawe 2008).

Box 4.12: Parents Under Pressure - module content

Modules   Comprehensive family assessment. Identification of targets
1 & 2:   for change.

Module 3: Challenging the notion of an ideal parent: aimed at strengthening the parents' perceptions of themselves as competent in the parenting role. Successes are added to a list of achievements in parent's workbook.

Module 4: How to parent under pressure - increasing mindful awareness: teaches skills involved in coping with negative emotional states using mindfulness techniques to tolerate negative emotional states without the need to avoid or escape them through the use of drugs.

Module 5: Connecting with your child and encouraging good behaviour: teaches traditional behavioural skills, including praise and reward to encourage good behaviour and child-centred play. Mindfulness techniques used to help parents focus on their children during play and increase their emotional availability.

Module 6: Mindful child management: teaches non-punitive child management techniques (eg time out). Mindfulness techniques include helping parents gain control over their own emotional responsivity in disciplinary situations aimed at reducing impulsive, emotion-driven punishment and increasing the effectiveness of techniques taught in module five.

Module 7: Coping with lapse and relapse: teaches skills to minimise the risk of lapses, emphasising prevention and mindful awareness of affective states that may be related to drug use (such as craving).

Module 8: Extending social networks: encourages parents to extend their support networks through the identification of potential sources of support.

Module 9: Life skills: includes practical advice on diet and nutrition, budgeting, health and exercise etc as needed.

Module 10: Relationships: aimed at improving effective communication between partners and identifying past unproductive relationship patterns.
(Harnett and Dawe 2008)

The Team Around the Child

The Team around the Child is a model that is being used widely by local authorities alongside the CAF - see Box 4.13 for a case study of one such model of The Team Around the Child being provided in Lambeth.[6] Although no published studies that explicitly examine this model of working are yet available, this general approach is consistent with policy recommendations. In Chapter Five we will examine some of the evidence around the benefits of integrated working models of this nature more generally.

---

6. For the full description from Lambeth see: www.lambeth.gov.uk/Services/EducationLearning/ TeamAroundTheChild/TACCaseStudyBradley.htm

Box 4.13: Team Around the Child case study: Bradley aged 10

This case study shows how a school initiated a CAF assessment and, when the case quickly escalated, used the CAF form as a referral to social care. The development of the TAC ran parallel to the initial assessment and supported the process, rather than duplicated it.

At a CAF surgery, a primary school inclusion manager and the TAC area manager discussed initiating a CAF assessment for 10-year-old Bradley. The boy's behaviour was deteriorating and school-based strategies were having little impact. The school also had concerns about his mother's possible alcohol-related issues and recent broken arm. They agreed to seek consent from Bradley's mother for an assessment to be completed in order to request the allocation of both a family support worker and a CAMHS early intervention worker.

Later that week, the school received a telephone call from social care advising them that a Schedule 1 offender was living with Bradley's mother and asking if the school had any concerns about the boy's eight-year-old sister 'B'. The school had no concerns about 'B' but relayed their concerns about Bradley, noting a link between the escalation in his behaviour and the Schedule 1 offender having moved into the family home. Social care had visited the offender, but neither the mother nor any children were home at the time.

The inclusion officer sent the completed CAF assessment to the TAC area manager and sent a copy to CAMHS. Aware that a Schedule 1 offender was now living with the family, a copy was also sent to social care (in place of the multiagency referral form).

A few days later, the headteacher attended a Locality Management Group meeting and told the TAC area manager of the call from social care. After the meeting the TAC area manager introduced the headteacher to the social inclusion safeguarding manager and the social care deputy team leader. A strategy meeting was held the following week attended by two social workers, a probation officer, the inclusion manager, the TAC area manager and the form teacher from the special school attended by Bradley's elder sister, 17-year-old 'A'.

In light of information shared at the meeting, it was agreed to initiate a Section 47 enquiry for all three children. It was also agreed that the CAF Action Plan for Bradley be implemented and a re-integration plan be developed as soon as possible, with high-level intervention from a family support worker to get Bradley back into school rather him be at home in the current circumstances. This fits with Section 47 enquiry guidance: 'Where necessary and appropriate, interim services and support must be provided to safeguard and promote the child's welfare until the Child Protection Conference is held.'

The TAC area manager also suggested to the special school teacher that serious consideration be given to initiating a CAF assessment for 'A's boyfriend 'L', who attended the same school and was closely linked to the Schedule 1 offender. There was clear evidence that both young people had significant additional needs and would benefit from multiagency support.

The inclusion manager, family support worker and TAC area manager met a few days later and agreed the re-integration process for Bradley. The family support worker would attend school every morning for the first week to support Bradley and his mother if she came into school, and would liaise with the CAMHS early intervention worker to arrange an assessment and intervention session at the school. As the initial Lead Professional, the inclusion manager liaised closely with the social worker to ensure they were working in partnership and sharing information.

Although it is beyond the remit of the current review, there is now a body of evidence pointing to the importance of providing child-focused treatments for children who have experienced abuse that incorporate 'knowledge of how maltreated youngsters negotiate stage-salient issues of development' (eg Cicchetti et al. 1988). Therapeutic interventions that are explicitly directed at the child should involve: a) an assessment of the child's social and emotional functioning in terms of the impact of the abuse on their capacity for security and trusting relationships; and b) work to help them address their attachment-related problems. Evidence from a recent systematic review shows that although there is very little evidence explicitly addressing therapeutic interventions for attachment disorder, the literature nevertheless shows benefits to the child-parent attachment relationship in biological families in the application of both psychoeducational and psychotherapeutic treatments (Cornell and Hamrin 2008).

4.4 Assessing change in parenting

Finally, decisions about ongoing packages of care that are provided as part of the Team Around the Child should be influenced not only by the profile of presenting problems but also by the patterns of change that have been observed across key domains of functioning in response to the implementation of a procedure to assess change (Harnett and Dawe 2008). These domains include parental psychological functioning, parenting skills, the parent-child relationship, family functioning and social context. In Chapter Three we examined recent research that pointed to the importance of assessing a parent's capacity to change, including an evaluation of their capacity to acquire parenting skills. Harnett and Dawe (2008), whose evaluation of the Parents Under Pressure programme was described above, suggest that this should include a number of steps (see Box 3.7 in Chapter Three), the final stage of which should involve an 'objective measurement of progress over time including standardised tests administered pre and post the intervention; direct observation of changes in parent-child interaction; and evaluation of the parents' willingness to engage and co-operate with the intervention and the extent to which targets were achieved' (Harnett and Dawe 2008). This process is consistent with the changes recommended in the Assessment Framework, and points to an urgent need for social workers in particular to begin to utilise the many available standardised tools as part of a broader approach to such assessment (see Chapter Three).

Summary of findings

> Support to families in which there are concerns about the safety of a child need to be underpinned by a partnership model of practice that is focused on goals and bringing about change in parenting capacity and the parent-child relationship; change should be assessed as part of the provision of intervention using a range of standardised instruments.

> There is no clear-cut research showing 'what works' with the type of families with whom social care services are primarily concerned. A number of recent reviews have, however, pointed to the importance of long-term 'relationship-based practice' with 'complex and resistant' families; there is also some evidence about the effectiveness of manualised programmes and they should as such be used as part of a broader approach underpinned by relationship-based working.

> New evidence from a range of disciplines including infant mental health, neuroscience and developmental psychology about early development point to the component factors of 'relationship-based' approaches that should be core to work with families; these findings also have implications in terms of the development of more effective communication with multidisciplinary colleagues.

> The research highlights the importance of an organisational context that facilitates 'relationship-based' and 'reflective' practice.

> The first three years of life should be a priority in terms of the provision of intervention and decision-making about the need to remove the child.

> Effective intervention during the first four years of life involves dyadic interventions including parent-infant/child psychotherapy, and should be provided by specialist practitioners.

> The Team Around the Child model appears to offer benefits in terms of both families and professionals (see Chapter Five for further discussion).

Chapter Six provides recommendations with regard to the provision of interventions at both a policy and practice level.

chapter five

Effective integrated working

This chapter:

> discusses in detail research about the different models of integrated working that have been identified, including models of integrated working in other European countries

> examines what the research suggests in terms of the factors that are now recognised to be hindering or facilitating the development of effective integrated working

> concludes with an examination of the evidence about the outcomes of integrated working.

5.1 Introduction

Following the Laming Inquiry in 2003 joint working was made a priority for children's services. The Children Act 2004 required local public bodies to work together through Children's Trusts, which most areas were expected to have in place by 2006, and all by 2008. However, the national Audit Commission (2008) found there was considerable local confusion about whether 'Children's Trust' meant a new statutory body or mandated partnership working.

Child protection services have faced problems with interagency collaboration since the 1960s, on issues such as 'lack of ownership amongst senior managers; inflexible organisational structures; conflicting professional ideologies; lack of budget control; communication problems; poor understanding of roles and responsibilities; and mistrust amongst professionals' (see Horwath and Morrison 2007 for an overview). Many of these problems have continued into recent times. They have been exacerbated by the fact that much of the current research fails to provide a common language to describe collaboration and by an absence of consistent messages about how to address the issues (Horwath and Morrison 2007).

A range of terms have been used to describe integrated working. These include holistic governance, joined-up working, multi- and cross-agency working, multi-professional/ disciplinary working, cross-boundary working, networks, collaboration and co-ordination (Percy-Smith 2006). Although some of these terms pertain to different levels of delivery, shared characteristics include the following:

> the structure and/or way of working involves two or more organisations.

> the organisations retain their own separate identities

> the relationship between the organisations is not that of contractor to provider

> there is some kind of agreement between the organisations to work together in pursuit of an agreed aim

> that aim could not be achieved, or is unlikely to be achieved, by any one organisation working alone

> relationships between organisations are formalised (ie partnership is more than a network) and are expressed through an organisational structure and the planning, implementation and review of an agreed programme of work (Percy-Smith 2006).

A number of different levels and degrees of service integration have been identified, ranging from low-level collaboration involving increased communication and co-operation, through to higher levels of collaboration involving co-ordination, coalition and ultimately integration. At the highest level of integration, there is a further distinction in terms of its application either to systems, administration or client-level concerns (Siraj-Blatchford and Siraj-Blatchford 2009). Furthermore, integration can occur across agencies within a single service sector (eg health, social services or education); across a population group (agencies providing different types of service); and within a particular service delivery organisation (Siraj-Blatchford and Siraj-Blatchford 2009).

It has been suggested that while integrated working is widely assumed to be a good thing it can be difficult to put into practice, and that its development 'requires careful planning, commitment and enthusiasm on the part of partners, the overcoming of organisational, structural and cultural barriers, and the development of new skills and ways of working' (Percy-Smith 2006).

In Chapter Two we introduced the concept of 'transdisciplinary working' to refer to a model in which members of different agencies work together jointly, sharing aims, information, tasks and responsibilities (Sloper 2004). This type of approach is explicitly centred on the needs of the child and family, with a Lead Practitioner (whose post is funded on a multiagency basis) playing a key role in designing and delivering a programme of care and co-ordinating services following a single co-ordinated multi-agency assessment. Sloper suggests this type of holistic approach would be rated most highly by families, but there was no clear indication at that point in time of the extent to which this model of working was being implemented.

In this chapter, we will highlight the findings from research that has been published since the Sloper (2004) review, about what works in relation to establishing and developing integrated working across a range of sectors and contexts. Service integration is defined as 'an ecological integrated children's system that is centred on the child and their family, served through service co-ordination, and supported through integrated organisations and agencies' (Siraj-Blatchford and Siraj-Blatchford 2009). We highlight research which suggests that what is important in terms of outcomes is 'quality' of integration rather than the 'type' of integration that is adopted, as well as research demonstrating the key aspects of successful collaborations.

5.2 Models of integrated working

One of the earliest studies that was conducted to identify common operational features found that integrated working appears to be developing as a two-stage process in which initial integrated working, based on strong personal relationships (localised integration), is followed by a second stage involving the creation of a fully integrated sustainable service based on professional relationships and supported by IT tools (mainstreamed integration) (Department for Children, Schools and Families 2007b). The typical characteristics, and structures and processes involved in mainstreamed integrated working are highlighted in Box 5.1.

Box 5.1: Typical characteristics and structures and processes involved in effective integrated working (Department for Children, Schools and Families 2007b).

Typical characteristics	Typical structures and processes
founded and sustained by very strong personal relationships between staff in co-located or locality teams	multiagency governance with representatives from all services and the community
deep commitment of staff; most have chosen to work in multiagency setting	multiagency management teams
no major dependence on IT, due to reliance on personal relationships	formal and informal multiagency networks provide support to service managers, front-line practitioners, key workers and those responsible for service co-ordination
high level of professional and personal support for staff	standardised referral processes with family consent for information sharing and providing feedback to referrers as integral part of process
strong leadership and management (vital)	common assessment used to support referrals into or out of service
integrated working principles embedded in strategic-level documents and communicated to all staff	weekly or bi-weekly multiagency allocation panels to handle referrals and allocate service[s] and/or a Lead Professional to the case
adoption of common models, language and service delivery approaches within the team	regular planning and case review meetings, often managed by the allocation panel and making use of standard forms and processes
effective information sharing within team and relevant external services, based on obtaining consent from family for information sharing at the outset	
use and benefits of shared facilities in relationship building, awareness raising, training and improving service delivery	
child and family at centre of provision re interventions, design and management of service	

Some of the common interventions that were used to develop and promote integrated working included the following:

> new induction processes designed to support practitioners in a multiagency environment

> training courses comprising multiagency staff, and awareness sessions run to provide all staff with basic understanding of other services

> effort put into ensuring staff were aware and kept up-to-date about services available in the local area

> carefully planned interventions to prepare staff for integrated working, prior to and after changes in structures or locations

> implementation of common processes for case review meetings, the CAF and Lead Professional, as part of an overall change programme

> involvement of staff in the development of new ways of working, and allowing service improvements to evolve (Department for Children, Schools and Families 2007b).

This study, which was undertaken in seven areas that had been nominated as examples of good practice, found that most of these areas were at the end of the first stage of integration. There was general recognition that further work was required to develop and broaden integrated working, and that it was too early to be able to measure impacts in terms of outcomes for children and young people.

More recently, the Audit Commission's (2008) review of Children's Trusts found that while almost all areas had revised the way in which children's services were co-ordinated, there was still substantial local variation, with little evidence that mainstream funding from social services, education and the NHS had been redirected or that performance had been managed across services. It is suggested that this explains the absence of improved outcomes for children and young people or improved value for money. The Audit Commission found that although primary care trusts, the police and schools feel they can influence the way Children's Trusts operate, there is less evidence of engagement by the voluntary and community sectors, and a need for better engagement on the part of individual schools.

The Audit Commission points to the need for 'substantial development' in Children's Trusts with better clarity between strategic, executive and operational issues and levels of working. It is suggested that Children's Trust Boards curently have little direct oversight of financial or budget matters, that performance management systems are underdeveloped, and that many representatives on Children's Trust Boards lack a mandate for committing their organisations' resources, and that systems for reporting back are rarely systematic.

The review also found that the early emphasis on pooled budgets had underestimated some of the practical difficulties of pooling funding in this way, including the fact that many partners would be reluctant to contribute money, as opposed to other resources. While many local agencies have aligned their financial, physical, and human resources, most pooling of budgets is only being successfully implemented between services that have 'a history of co-operation that often predates local Children's Trust arrangements' (Audit Commission 2008).

This finding is confirmed by research about expenditure on children's services across 35 Children's Trust pathfinders, combined with an in-depth analysis of local authorities and primary care trusts across eight pathfinder areas and three non-pathfinder areas (Lorgelly et al. 2009). This showed that local authorities and NHS trusts had co-ordinated expenditure in a range of ways (eg informal agreements and aligning budgets), but pooling of budgets was mostly used for selected services (eg CAMHS). Only four trusts pooled the budgets across all children's services. The authors conclude: 'Sharing money for local children's services requires shared objectives, trust, and legal and accounting expertise. Several different mechanisms are permitted and many are feasible but programme budgeting for children's services could make them more effective.'

The Audit Commission's findings are also confirmed by another recent review of effective practice in integrating early years services, which highlights a number of areas for action by local decision-makers and managers, and also for regional and national decision-makers. It concludes that the development of multidisciplinary and interdisciplinary approaches to the delivery of services should now be treated as a priority (Siraj-Blatchford and Siraj-Blatchford 2009). The recommendations of these two major reviews are summarised in Boxes 5.2 and 5.3. There is also some suggestion of the need for agreed working and pay structures in multiagency teams, and better clarification about the sources of continued funding for service integration, as well as the need to ensure that staffing levels match caseload demands. The need for greater clarification of the roles and responsibilities associated with the roles of Lead Professional and 'key worker' are also identified.

Box 5.2: Areas for action for regional and national decision-makers

1. An updated single source of future guidance comprising:

> a clear vision of service integration to be disseminated and promoted to staff at all levels

> a common definition of 'commissioning' for local government, the NHS and the police

> clarification of the core objectives of the Every Child Matters policy to address the tension that some stakeholders see between the needs of families and children, and to make the roles of universal, targeted and preventative services clear

> an overall (interdisciplinary) strategy for service assessment and intervention, which also provides a common language

> agreement on service thresholds and tiers of need

> consistent, cross-departmental support to local collaborative working between Children's Trusts, Local Strategic Partnerships and other thematic partnerships

2. Alignment of financial accounting and performance reporting frameworks to make it easier for local public bodies to understand one another's contributions and challenges, and align resources locally; creation of opportunities for appropriate financial processes (aligning or pooling) as opposed to prescription

3. Better provision for workforce development nationally and regionally to support effective integrated delivery in the early years services

4. More robust research that addresses the evidence gaps, including the identification and promotion of agreed outcome measures and standardised research instruments

5. Procedures to enable the newly created Centre for Excellence and Outcomes in Children and Young People's Services (C4EO) to support Children's Trusts by benchmarking performance and sharing good practice. (Adapted from Audit Commission 2008 and Siraj-Blatchford and Siraj-Blatchford 2009)

> **Box 5.3: Areas for action by local managers**
>
> 1. Clarification of the objectives of integrated working for all those involved in service management and delivery
>
> 2. Development of an approach to service assessment and intervention that provides:
>
> > recognition of the additional burdens of integrated working in terms of, for example, the completion of CAF forms, duties of the Lead Professional, etc
>
> > a common language and greater agreement on service thresholds and tiers of need
>
> > clarification about continued funding for service integration
>
> > engagement of 'missing partners' in Children's Trusts, including voluntary sector organisations and families
>
> > self-assessment questions that can be used to improve working (see Appendix B)
>
> 3. Training at all levels to develop:
>
> > leadership for integrated services
>
> > a shared philosophy and vision
>
> > better communication systems
>
> > a clear staff review and supervision system
>
> > shared understanding of roles
>
> 4 Training of service co-ordinators to ensure they have an adequate knowledge of the full range of services available in supporting the Every Child Matters agenda
>
> 5 Review of current governance and management arrangements for children's services, to focus on delivering improved outcomes. (Adapted from Audit Commission 2008 and Siraj-Blatchford and Siraj-Blatchford 2009)

The literature on models of integrated working is diverse and in a recent review of the findings about theories and models published since 2000, Robinson, Atkinson and Downing (2008a; 2008b) organised the evidence in terms of four criteria:

1. the extent of integration (ie the stage or depth of collaborative activity in integrated services)

2. the integration of structures in terms of the layers of an organisation's functions (eg governance and strategic levels and front-line operational service delivery levels)

3. the integration of processes in terms of the ordering of work activities across time and place, at different organisational levels

4. and reach in terms of the extent to which diverse agencies are included.

The findings in relation to each of these four criteria are discussed in detail below.

In terms of the **extent of integration**, the authors conclude that key features of this criterion include factors such as the presence of shared responsibility and ownership, mutual dependency, sustainability, joint planning, communication and information exchange, and integration of structures and processes, and that these features could be used to examine the extent to which integration has become embedded. Issues raised by increasing the extent of integration relate to the loss of autonomy for individual partners or agencies, with risks in terms of resources and reputation. Where integration hasn't been achieved, key concerns focus on the reliance on key individuals and lack of sustainability. The review also found some indication that more advanced integration resulted in 'greater burdens on those involved in terms of partnership development and the time and resources required' although it is suggested that these problems need to be balanced against the associated benefits. It is also suggested that 'there appears to have been a move away from the view of integrated services as the ideal model, towards a view that the outcomes of integrated working are situation specific and that diverse approaches to the degree or extent of integration may be equally valid'.

In terms of the **integration of key structures**, the review concludes that more than one level of integration is needed and that integration is multi-layered. At the macro level, tensions are due to divergences between key policy models such as Every Child Matters and the National Service Framework. Integration is also heterogeneous and there is potential for considerable variation at different levels - for example, in terms of the position of service user/community (eg as recipient or co-participant), applicability to a particular context (eg whether it is applied to all children's services or services targeting specific groups or just time-limited projects), and the extent to which change management is utilised. Key challenges at a strategic level include barriers to pooling budgets under current guidance, tensions between the integrative model and individual agency models, and barriers in terms of front-line joint working, which include, for example, unsuitable buildings, agency commitment, sustainability, staff terms and conditions, and unrealistic timescales. Enablers include flexibility or responsiveness with regard to policy and local development, time for capacity building, and at a strategic level, the relating of organisational structure to purposeful planning and leadership, and a focus on outcomes.

In terms of the **integration of processes**, this study found three recurring themes - change management processes, routine or procedural system processes, and interprofessional joint activities. The findings suggest a need for transformation of processes involving skills, knowledge 'and practice of the workforce' and that key leadership skills, in terms of senior managers at strategic levels, are needed to support distributed processes of network building, consensus building and reflective decision-making. The review also suggests that at an operational front-line level, important management skills for securing effective interprofessional working include managing interdisciplinary relationships and supervision, and that different models of front-line working have implications for professionals' work processes around role clarification - for example, in terms of new roles such as Lead Professionals and how such roles fit within the different service tiers. In terms of assessment and information sharing, the challenges highlighted include time and training and the involvement of users; in terms of referrals and establishing extended roles, challenges include restrictive eligibility criteria and confidentiality; and in terms of interprofessional process, they include confronting cultural differences. Strategic level enablers include continuity of personnel and career pathways, and at an operational level include the development of effective information sharing systems, shared goals and tasks, and retention of key specialisms when roles change.

Finally, in terms of the **reach of integration**, the findings show that the development of partnership working in children's services has involved agencies and organisations of varying size and status (including the voluntary sector) in more direct working and decision-making relationships with the major departments of national and local government, with implications in terms of power relations, and gradually extending to include the involvement of users as partners or participants in the process.
It is suggested that at a governance level, 'some boards appear to be better suited to successfully managing and capitalising on this wider inclusion by encouraging and enabling new priorities to emerge and respecting the values of other partners'. At an operational level, the authors suggest that 'the perspectives and goals of less powerful partners may be overridden by the internal priorities of fund-holding agencies, leading

to a failure to exploit their potential contributions or even their withdrawal'. In cases where it is not possible to widen inclusion in partnerships, alternative means of involving some groups in decision-making are necessary. Further issues include partnership and participation, the beneficial outcomes of widening inclusion in partnership (such as increased accessibility of services and increased trust within the partnership) and, indeed, the potential for a negative impact of wider partnership in terms of accountability, both horizontally between partners and vertically in terms of established procedures for accountability and modes of governance.

European models

Research examining models of integrated working in European countries has highlighted a number of important factors. One practice-based research project that explored health and welfare services across 12 European countries (Katz and Hetherington 2006), distinguishing between approaches that are child and family-welfare focused (Nordic countries) and those that are child protection focused (English-speaking countries), found evidence of better integration in countries utilising holistic, family-welfare focused systems.

Katz and Hetherington identified a range of innovative strategies used in European countries to promote co-operation and different ways to overcome boundaries and encourage communication (see Box 5.4). In Sweden, for example, the highest level of integration was observed with child welfare services provided by the local authority social services department, which also provides community-based mental health services. The local authorities also run the state health service, creating a strong connection between health and social services at a higher management level. Co-operation with voluntary organisations is commonplace. Other Nordic countries also showed high levels of integration, with some districts in Norway having permanent interdisciplinary teams based in schools with representatives from nursery schools, the health services and child protection agencies. Similarly, in Denmark health visitors and social workers are co-located within the same building and hold regular weekly joint meetings.

> **Box 5.4: European strategies to enhance co-operation between agencies and professions**
>
> **Denmark** Health visitors and social workers occupy the next floor of the same building as the child welfare social workers and they hold weekly meetings.
>
> **Norway** Permanent school-based multidisciplinary teams, with representatives from nursery schools, the health services and child protection agencies, are based in schools.
>
> **France** Regular multidisciplinary team meetings of the local authority child health and welfare services are attended by the sector social workers, child health paediatricians and nurses, specialist child welfare social workers and psychologists, and involve collective decision-making.
>
> **Italy** Regular monthly meetings between community child and maternal health service (including health and social work professionals), and the hospital based maternity services. Cases brought for discussion for learning purposes rather than decision-making, and to promote trust between professionals and agencies.
> (Katz and Hetherington 2006)

This research found that most other European countries invested more money than the UK in preventative stages of work and have better resourced child welfare services (see Box 5.5).

Box 5.5: European child welfare services

'Services such as intensive family support teams with well qualified workers, child mental health services, flexible foster care (weekend, weekday, short-term respite care) and residential child care, or counselling for abused children, were available without long waiting lists. Lack of communication might mean that a family was faced with too many different services, but was less likely to mean that they got no service.' (Katz and Hetherington 2006)

By inviting feedback from professionals on a likely outcome for a vignette that depicted a family with escalating problems culminating in severe mental illness and very serious child protection issues, the researchers found that the countries with the best outcomes 'were those where the professionals refused to accept that the final stage would have happened, either because they considered that their intervention would have prevented the escalation or because they felt that the community would have stepped in'. The authors suggest this points to the importance of both good resources and strong communities.

Two key themes appeared repeatedly and cross-nationally: the need to work together with other agencies, and to maintain a focus on the family as a whole. The authors suggest this involves a wide network of services. The research highlighted a number of ways of fostering interagency co-operation, including formal reporting protocols, technological data exchanges, informal meetings, multidisciplinary teams, co-location of services, joint training and interagency strategic bodies.

The research also shows three underlying principles that not only foster better interagency collaboration but better engagement with children and families - trust, authority and negotiation (Katz and Hetherington 2006), of which trust was the most important.

> *Trust was engendered by professionals who had the authority to make decisions and who felt empowered to help the family. The mode of interaction between these workers and families (and inter-professionally) was to engage in negotiations - implying that each party had something to contribute.*

These include some of the underlying principles of the relationship and partnership-based model of working that has been core to the discussion throughout this publication.

Box 5.6: The importance of the orientation of the system

'Although structural, technological and organisational factors can influence productive sharing of information between practitioners, these factors are secondary to a more fundamental issue: that is, whether the basic orientation of the system is to focus on risk or support. Where the underlying focus is on risk, it may be harder to build a culture that validates the authority of practitioners to exercise judgement and that values the time spent on communication. Services that are successful in improving collaboration and communication encourage the building of relationships (between workers and families and between workers in different agencies). Provision of resources and time for both formal and informal communication between practitioners from different agencies and professions is a priority for making integration work.' (Katz and Hetherington 2006)

A further recent study examining European perspectives on social work (Boddy and Statham 2009) found that multiagency and multidisciplinary team working is most effective where it is underpinned by clarity concerning the particular contribution of each agency or service, and also 'respect for each other's specific expertise, rather than an attempt to do away with difference and blur professional boundaries' (Boddy and Statham 2009).

Other models

A number of possible models of integrated working have been highlighted (eg Thoburn 2009). These include:

> a 'team around the child and family' (Burton 2009; Siraj-Blatchford, Clarke and Needham 2007).

> a single worker with a very small caseload and 24-hour availability of supervision or consultation, as for example in intensive family preservation models developed in the US that have been adapted for use in the UK (eg Tunstill et al 2009; Cabinet Office 2007; Brandon and Connolly 2006).

> a co-working model derived from family therapy in which two workers share the Lead Professional role for the family as a whole (Thoburn 2009).

In terms of social care, Hackney's 'Reclaiming Social Work', which is currently being evaluated, involves the development of Social Work Units that replace individual caseloads with teams consisting of a consultant social worker, qualified social worker, children's practitioner, half-time family therapist and an administrator, who jointly work on cases together. The work of the team is overseen by senior managers, and staff are offered training in other skills such as family therapy.

This type of model is consistent with those that have been developed in Europe. However, although social workers in the UK are increasingly working in multiprofessional teams, one of the key differences between England and other European countries is the level of professional qualification of the other workers in the core children's services team (Boddy and Statham 2009). In France, for example, the teams that provide services for children and families commonly include social workers, social pedagogues, psychologists and specialists in child and family law. Boddy and Statham's research suggests that in European countries, social workers not only have a role as part of specialist services where there are issues in terms of the need for placements away from home, but also as part of the type of multidisciplinary teams referred to above, which are based in universal settings such as schools and family centres. One of the conclusions of Chapters Three and Four is the need to have infant/child psychotherapists as core members of these specialist teams across all levels of safeguarding.

5.3 What hinders and facilitates joined-up working?

One of the earliest reviews of the evidence on integrated working to identify factors that hinder or facilitate co-ordinated multiagency services (Sloper 2004) identified the importance of having: clear aims, roles and responsibilities including clear lines of accountability; agreed timetables between partners for the implementation of changes, including an incremental approach to change; strong leadership and a multiagency steering or management group; commitment at all levels of the organisations involved, in addition to involvement of front-line staff in development of policies; good systems of communication and information sharing (including IT systems); support and training for staff in new ways of working; and interprofessional programmes of continuing education.

More recently the NfER review of the evidence (Robinson, Atkinson and Downing 2008a; 2008b) identified enablers and challenges at a number of levels. Challenges emanating from contextual barriers and political climate included changes in political steer, financial uncertainty, agency reorganisations and the organisational change climate. Organisational challenges that were identified related primarily to agencies having different policies, procedures and systems that do not blend. Cultural and professional obstacles included 'tendencies toward negative assessment and professional stereotyping' alongside different professional beliefs. Other challenges that were highlighted included that of ensuring commitment and involving children and families.

Enablers of integrated working that were identified in this review focused on the following five areas:

1. Clarity of purpose/recognised need

> clarity for stakeholders about the basis of involvement and the need for this in terms of resources, avoiding duplication, meeting key aims

> the establishment of a coherent and clear long-term vision and a focus on compatible goals

> common aims and collective ownership of shared goals

> clarity around shared objectives

2. Commitment at all levels

> commitment to the vision of integration throughout organisations through, for example, the provision of resources and support at a strategic level

> buy-in to core concepts and senior strategic management ownership of the vision, and pooled budgets to ensure it works

> the capacity of boards to give strategic leadership and creation of collaborative capacity at a strategic level

3. Strong leadership and management

> supportive leadership to establish and model the 'emotional tone' including awareness of the emotional processes around change and creation of systems to manage the consequences of change

> emotional labour and emotional intelligence in management and leadership roles associated with the development of partnerships

> dedicated posts for developing capacity for change and establishing inclusive change management processes

4. Relationships/trust between partners

> strong personal relationships, trust and respect including trust between professional groups, sharing of skills and expertise, willingness to be honest about knowledge gaps

> reflection on process in terms of working relationships and processes and need for feedback to strengthen collaborative relationships

> processes to manage ambiguity and conflict, promote trust and contain anxiety between partners

> a realistic time frame

> need for joined-up attitude involving trust, a self-reflective attitude and enthusiasms for collaborative working

> a history of working together and early positive experiences of collaboration

5. Understanding/clarity of roles and responsibilities

> for example, of the role of the Lead Professional, which may vary across local authorities

> solid professional identities and clear roles
> flexibility - this requires relationships to be less hierarchical and roles
  to be dependent on needs of organisation, situation, professional colleagues,
  the client and the family, as well as professional training
> strong sense of values and allegiances
> reciprocal respect regardless of formal status
> involvement of relevant people, effective structures, systems and procedures
> good communication and joint training
> restructuring - this should follow careful consideration of three factors: the needs of
  children; the types of services required to meet those needs; and the experience and
  skills required of staff, along with their physical location (reliance on restructuring
  alone is inadequate) (Robinson, Atkinson and Downing 2008a; 2008b).

Worrall-Davies and Cottrell (2009) have also highlighted from the current literature
the commonly recognised pre-requisites for effective integrated working (Box 5.7),
and commonly recognised barriers (Box 5.8) citing the work of Anning et al. (2006),
whose study of multiprofessional working in children's services identified four areas
to be addressed: 'structural issues (coping with systems/management change);
ideological issues (the sharing and redistribution of knowledge/skills/beliefs);
procedural (participation and reification in delivering services) and interprofessional
(the need to learn through role change)'.

These findings suggest there is now considerable clarity, both in terms of children's
services and more generally, about the key factors that facilitate or hinder integrated
working, and that these now need to be addressed in practice.

Box 5.7: Prerequisites for effective integrated working

> commitment to joint working at all levels of the organisations, from senior
  managers to grassroots practitioners
> strategic and operational joint planning and commissioning
> service level agreements and clear interagency protocols cutting across
  procedural bureaucracy
> clear, jointly agreed aims, objectives and timetables for the service
> delineation of roles and responsibilities for all staff and clarity of line-
  management arrangements
> mutual trust and respect between partner agencies and staff
> recognition of the constraints others are under
> good systems of communication and good relationships at grassroots level
> clear paths for information sharing, including databases
> support, supervision and joint training for staff in new way of working
> secondments between services - services co-existing in one building
> commitment to evaluation, audit and change
> commitment to consulting with and acting on user/carer views.
  (Worrall-Davies and Cottrell 2009)

Box 5.8: Factors preventing effective integrated working

> previous 'history' of conflict between individuals and organisations

> competitive relationships between services

> bureaucratic need to follow agency procedures, which may lead to stifled creative planning

> accountability issues - lack of clarity about who takes responsibility in each agency and dysfunction at both operational and strategic levels

> professionals and disciplines insisting on undertaking particular parts of assessments and therapeutic work

> interdisciplinary power struggles

> lack of a 'common language'. (Worrall-Davies and Cottrell 2009)

5.4 Outcomes of effective integrated working

In Chapter Three we presented the findings from the Local Authorities Research Consortium about the outcomes of the CAF using a four-tier impact model that distinguished between change to input processes; change to routines, experiences and attitudes; changes in outcomes; and changes in terms of institutional systemic embedding. In this section we focus on the outcomes of integrated working more generally.

The most recent evidence about the outcome of integrated children's services comes from the evaluation of England's Children's Trust pathfinders (O'Brien et al. 2009), which were established in 2003 to promote greater integration in children's services. This research found that although there was no consistent quantitative evidence of improved outcomes, 25 of the 35 trusts provided evidence of the Children's Trust pathfinder arrangements improving outcomes for children. Examples of improved outcomes are provided for both individual and groups of children, and include better networking and co-ordination between different agencies, and improved mechanisms for the flexible use of funds, such as the pooling of health and social care funds (see Box 5.9). However, the authors note that the extent and nature of beneficial outcomes identified was limited by the fact that much of the work was 'still at its early phase of implementation at the end of the evaluation period' and 'key practical components of the programme were not fully in place'. The research also found that those Children's Trust pathfinders that were focusing their attention on 'all children' or 'all vulnerable children' showed the most progress (ie compared with trusts focusing on selected groups of children, such as those with mental health needs). The authors note, however, that some trusts may have had stronger 'embryonic environments to take on the challenge' in terms of having a 'legacy of better child outcomes' prior to the introduction of pathfinders, or that other unobserved features in terms of the type of integration introduced, may also have played a role.

> Box 5.9: Examples of improved group case outcomes provided by Children's Trust pathfinders in 2006
>
> > 'By streamlining referral pathways and introducing a key worker scheme we have significantly reduced the length of time from identification or diagnosis to the right services being involved. Families report being better able to cope and more in control. The number of families using support services has significantly increased. It is too early to be confident about trends and there is a complex mix of variables but the early signs are that improved services and quicker access to services is reducing the number of children entering care because of pressures arising from the child's disability.'
>
> > 'The inclusion of young people with disabilities in an integrated inclusive children's centre means they are able to access a full range of services including child care. This includes access to specialist nursing support for things like tube feeding.'
>
> > 'Funding through the local public service agreement secured the appointment of five additional speech and language therapists. This enables one therapist to be allocated five mainstream primary schools and the opportunity for significant project work in secondary schools where there had previously been no service.'
>
> > 'An outreach service commissioned by the Children's Trust improved the economic well-being of a number of families within the areas as it was able to get in touch with a number of the harder to reach families who frequently had not been claiming the benefits they were entitled to.'
>
> > 'We have increased numbers of children and young people receiving services. This has resulted in positive feedback from young people.'
>
> > 'We have reduced waiting lists for therapies by increasing early intervention.'
> > (O'Brien et al. 2009)

These findings are consistent with those of a recent review commissioned by the NfER to bring together studies about integrated working, which identified impacts for service users, professionals and services (Robinson, Atkinson and Downing 2008a; 2008b). These included the following:

1. Impact for service users:

> improved access to services and speedier response

> better information and communication from professionals

> increasing involvement of services users and wider communities

> holistic approach

> improved outcomes eg maintenance in home setting and improvement in attainment.

2. Impact for professionals:

> better understanding of the issues and children's needs

> increased understanding and trust between professionals

> greater willingness to take risks and potential for innovation and improved outcomes

> co-learning eg sharing skills, understanding and awareness

> increased demands and pressures on individual agencies

> joined-up working an 'add-on' to existing workload

> insufficient time for negotiation and information exchange

> lack of adequate administrative support.

3. Impact for services:

3.1 quality

> improved service-user experience (eg reduced multiple assessments, more responsiveness, improved access to specialist services, reduced waiting times, better information and advocacy, empowered children and families) and more seamless services

> clearer identification of service gaps, improved integration and overcoming of fragmentation

> involvement of community and service-users

> harnessing of resources of individual partners.

3.2 efficiency

> elimination of contradictions or tensions between policies, programmes and interventions, which improves deployment of resources by eliminating duplication, sharing of overheads, securing better value for money and achievement of economies

> impact on broader social policy objectives eg devolution of solution development through promotion of local problem-solving based on local needs analysis

> building of capacity to resolve policy problems through additional resources or flow of ideas and co-operation between stakeholders.

3.3 others

> greater focus on prevention and early intervention

> greater reliance on evidence-based practice thereby focusing on targeting conditions that affect families and communities' ability to care for children (Robinson, Atkinson and Downing 2008a; 2008b).

Summary of findings

Models of working

The findings suggest that integrated working is taking place as part of a two-stage process, the first of which (localised integration) involves reliance on strong personal relationships, and the second of which (mainstreamed integration) involves a fully sustainable service. However, the research suggests that few areas have achieved the second stage, and highlights particular problems in the development of Children's Trusts in terms of a failure to pool budgets, an absence of engagement with the voluntary sector, lack of mandate on the part of board members, and absence of performance management systems and oversight of budgets. Areas for action by local managers and regional or national decision-makers have been highlighted (Boxes 5.2 and 5.3).

A review of the evidence about theories and models of working highlights four key areas, and suggests that these should be used to examine what has been achieved:

1. the extent of integration (eg stage or depth of collaborative activity in integrated services)

2. integration of structures in terms of the layers of an organisation's functions (eg governance and strategic levels versus front-line operational service delivery levels)

3. the integration of processes in terms of the ordering of work activities across time and place, at different organisational levels

4. and reach in terms of the extent to which diverse agencies are included.

Evidence from studies examining European models of working shows that the highest level of integration has occurred in Nordic countries where there is a high level of commitment to the implementation of a holistic, child-welfare model of organisation (ie as opposed to a child protection approach), characterised by higher levels of investment and better resourced child welfare services.

A number of social care models of working have been highlighted including:

> a 'team around the child and family'

> a single worker with a very small caseload and 24-hour availability of supervision or consultation (as, for example, in intensive family preservation models developed in the US that have been adapted for use in the UK)

> a co-working model derived from family therapy in which two workers share the Lead Professional role for the family as a whole

> and Social Work Units (Hackney Reclaiming Social Work).

Although social workers in the UK are increasingly working as part of multidisciplinary teams of this nature, there is a key difference in terms of the level of professional qualification of the other workers in core children's services teams, with English teams lacking the level of expertise seen in other European countries. The research on European models of working also shows more differentiation within the social work role, with social workers playing a key part in transdisciplinary teams at other service levels (eg universal and targeted services).

Research on successful European models suggests that the basis for effective integration lies not only in the fostering of interagency co-operation using tools such as joint training and interagency strategic bodies, but in the three underlying principles of trust, authority and negotiation. These are some of the underlying principles of the relationship and partnership-based model of working discussed in Chapter Two.

Factors that hinder and facilitate integrated working

The research identifies four areas that need to be addressed in terms of prerequisites for and barriers to effective integrated working:

1. structural issues (coping with systems/management change)

2. ideological issues (the sharing and redistribution of knowledge/skills/beliefs)

3. procedural issues (participation and reification in delivering services)

4. and inter-professional issues (the need to learn through role change)

(Worrall-Davies and Cottrell 2009).

Significant enablers of integrated working that have been highlighted include: i) clarity of purpose/recognised need; ii) commitment at all levels; iii) strong leadership and management; iv)relationships/trust between partners; v) understanding/clarity of roles and responsibilities.

Factors preventing integrated working include a history of conflict; competition between services; bureaucratic need to follow agency procedures; accountability issues (in terms of a lack of clarity about who takes responsibility in each agency); professionals insisting on undertaking particular parts of assessment or provision of intervention; interdisciplinary power struggles; and the lack of a common language.

Outcomes of integrated working

Overall, the research suggests that integrated working is providing benefits and improved outcomes at a number of levels. The evidence is still very limited, however, in terms of quantitative measures of improvements in children's well-being, and this reflects the fact that integrated working is still not embedded particularly in terms of Children's Trusts and that the focus should now be on taking this forward.

chapter six

Discussion

6.1 Introduction

In this section we bring together our vision of a 21st century model of safeguarding, by drawing out some of the key messages from the range of published papers and documents that we identified, which addressed the questions raised at the outset (see Chapter One). Although much of the discussion has been informed by evidence from rigorously conducted research, we have where necessary based our conclusions on knowledge secured from discussion papers and books. For example, while some of the conceptual issues are very firmly underpinned by a widely developed evidence base (such as the importance of the first three years of life and children's social and emotional development), some of the concepts (such as, for example, complexity and critical realism) are the culmination of wide-ranging discussions and consensus opinion.

The key messages in this publication are consistent with the policy context for safeguarding that has been developed over the past decade, which has begun the process of moving away from a child protection to a child-welfare model of safeguarding (Gilbert et al. 2009a). This policy move has brought the UK into alignment with our European counterparts (Katz and Hetherington 2006), although there is still much more that we can learn from them in terms of integrated working, investment, and training (Boddy and Statham 2009).

The policy context for moving toward a child-welfare model of working, which emphasises the delivery of family support across all levels of provision (ie from universal level through to specialist services), is now largely in place. Three of the key findings of this report are:

1. The practices arising from revised policy are more favourable to both families and practitioners, and there is early evidence of better outcomes.

2. There is, nevertheless, a significant gap between such policy and actual provision on the ground, and a need for considerable change to practice to bring it into alignment with policy.

3. There is a need for further changes to practice that go beyond the policy recommendations that have been made to date.

Although we recognise the lead role and professional responsibility of social workers with regard to safeguarding, the findings of this report are of relevance to all practitioners working across the safeguarding continuum.

The next section examines the overall model that is suggested by both policy and research, and the second section examines the recommendations at strategic, operational and practitioner level.

6.2 An evidence-based 21st century model of safeguarding

Every Child Matters and the *Framework for the Assessment of Children in Need and their Families* have created the necessary policy context for a 21st century model of safeguarding. However, the research suggests that further changes are now needed, and supports the model of provision depicted in Figure 6.1.

At Level 1 (see Figure 6.1):

1. A public health model of safeguarding recognises that harm to children occurs along a continuum (ie ranging from not at all, mild, moderate, to very severe). A recent study showed that improved practices, in terms of the provision of parenting support training across the entire childcare workforce, produced large improvements in three independently derived population indicators of child abuse (Prinz et al. 2009).

   Recent evidence from infant mental health and neuroscience has pointed to the importance of the first three years of life in terms of the child's developing neurological system and in particular their brain. Research in the field of developmental psychology has similarly indicated the importance of this period in terms of the child's capacity for developing secure attachment relationships, with 'disorganised attachment' (which is strongly associated with later psychopathology) being present in up to 80 per cent of maltreated populations.

   Taken together, this research points to the importance of supporting high-risk families during the perinatal period, and of effective links between practitioners working at all levels of the safeguarding system, including the need for an increased use of the CAF, which provides the basis for more effective working across the different service levels.

   This research also points to the importance of intervening to remove babies and toddlers much earlier than has been achieved to date where intervention is not proving effective in improving their early environment.

2. Recent evidence shows that few children who experience maltreatment come to the attention of child protection agencies, and that the prevalence of maltreatment is in fact much higher than has been recognised to date (around 10 per cent based on data obtained from large normal population-based studies). It is beyond the scope of social services professionals to address this level of maltreatment, much of which could be effectively dealt with through the implementation of wider family support.

   Furthermore, analysis of the data on child deaths and serious injury through abuse and neglect shows that just under half of the children were under four years of age, and that the families of young children who sustained physical assaults (including head injuries) were in contact with universal or adult services, not children's social care.

   The research suggests that continuity of contact provided by professionals in schools, and in a range of other universal settings (eg children centres, primary care) provide important opportunities to improve recognition of, response to, and support of children who are experiencing abuse. Many settings in which there are key opportunities to identify and support such children are not being used for such purposes, and research examining European methods of integrated working suggest a number of innovative models of working (see below).

3. International research confirms that the holistic model of working that is implemented in Nordic countries, and that promotes the implementation of early intervention and preventive work, results in more effectively integrated services. These countries highlight the benefits of developing new ways of integrating services and of working co-operatively to promote child welfare across traditional service boundaries. International research has also highlighted the range of specialist professionals that work as part of multidisciplinary teams in other countries (Boddy and Statham 2009) and suggests the need for greater differentiation of the social work workforce to enable them to develop new roles within community-based teams. This research points to the importance of: i) developing standard multipractice teams across a) perinatal services, b) children's centres, and c) schools; and ii) the need for social workers to work as an integral part of such teams alongside other specialists, such as parent-infant/child psychotherapists (see Figure 6.1).

At Level 2

4. The continued focus of professionals on whether or not to 'report' suspected child maltreatment, and the failure to implement the CAF more widely, mean that significant levels of maltreatment that could be effectively dealt with through additional family support, go unidentified and that families go unsupported at the point at which it is most needed.

In terms of children with additional needs, the research points to the benefit of transdisciplinary Team Around the Child models of working that incorporate both statutory and voluntary sector services alongside partnership working with the family and child (see Figure 6.1).

At Level 3

5. The findings also suggest that despite the refocusing initiative and subsequent policies, social services departments are still focusing predominantly on managing 'risk'. This has resulted in the development of a risk filtration system with the consequences being the early closure of cases 'in need' and much service provision being confined to families in which there is an absence of concerns about parenting. Child investigations are also still viewed as the best way of securing services for families, despite an increasing body of evidence suggesting that initial assessments followed by the provision of services are more acceptable to families and can produce better outcomes.

The evidence points to the benefits of new transdisciplinary models of working, in terms of children with complex needs, in which the social worker leads a team of specialists that includes a family therapist and child psychotherapist/psychologist (see 'models of working' in the key recommendations below).

Figure 6.1: 21st century model of safeguarding

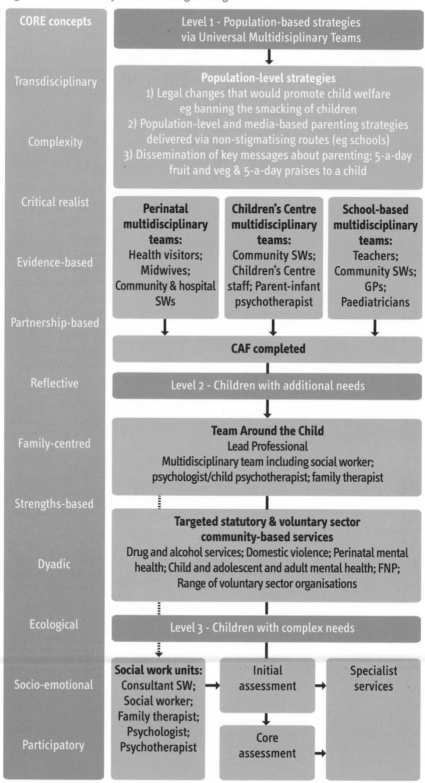

CORE concepts	
	Level 1 - Population-based strategies via Universal Multidisiplinary Teams
Transdisciplinary	**Population-level strategies** 1) Legal changes that would promote child welfare eg banning the smacking of children 2) Population-level and media-based parenting strategies delivered via non-stigmatising routes (eg schools) 3) Dissemination of key messages about parenting: 5-a-day fruit and veg & 5-a-day praises to a child
Complexity	
Critical realist	**Perinatal multidisciplinary teams:** Health visitors; Midwives; Community & hospital SWs / **Children's Centre multidisciplinary teams:** Community SWs; Children's Centre staff; Parent-infant psychotherapist / **School-based multidisciplinary teams:** Teachers; Community SWs; GPs; Paediatricians
Evidence-based	
Partnership-based	**CAF completed**
Reflective	**Level 2 - Children with additional needs**
Family-centred	**Team Around the Child** Lead Professional Multidisciplinary team including social worker; psychologist/child psychotherapist; family therapist
Strengths-based	**Targeted statutory & voluntary sector community-based services** Drug and alcohol services; Domestic violence; Perinatal mental health; Child and adolescent and adult mental health; FNP; Range of voluntary sector organisations
Dyadic	
Ecological	**Level 3 - Children with complex needs**
Socio-emotional	**Social work units:** Consultant SW; Social worker; Family therapist; Psychologist; Psychotherapist → Initial assessment → Specialist services
Participatory	Core assessment →

102

6.3 Key recommendations

The following recommendations apply across the safeguarding continuum and at all three levels in terms of the model depicted in Figure 6.1:

At strategic level
Policy

The issues and recommendations below should be addressed during the next stage of policy development.

> The concepts discussed in Chapter Two should be made central to safeguarding policy documents.

> Greater emphasis should be given to the importance of pregnancy and the first three years of life as being the foundation for a child's later well-being; in terms of prevention and early intervention, safeguarding should focus on the first three years.

> Assessment of families (including the identification of families in which there is high risk of harm) should take place as early as possible and universal level services are the ideal place for this to occur, particularly those on offer during pregnancy and the postnatal period (see Department of Health and Department for Children, Schools and Families 2008); the progressive universalism underpinning the Healthy Child Programme provides the necessary policy context for early identification of families about whom there are safeguarding concerns; the CAF is the key mechanism for securing additional services where there are concerns during this period; the first few years of life are not only optimal in terms of a child's development, they are also the optimal time to remove a child where the family are not able to change in response to the services being offered.

> There is a need to establish:

> > transdisciplinary teams including social workers as integral members, as part of: i) perinatal services; ii) children's centres; and iii) schools (see Level 1 of Figure 6.1)

> > infant mental health services consisting of parent-infant and child psychotherapists who have the specialist expertise to work with high-risk families, both during pregnancy and the first two to three years of life, and who are employed to support the work of the above perinatal and children's centre teams.

> The parent-child relationship and parenting capacity should be given greater emphasis in the assessment process, and should be primary in decision-making both about the provision of services and the need to remove the child from the home (see Box 3.5); moderating effects, such as the child's parentability, should be incorporated into the assessment of parenting capacity, and the presence of disability, illness or emotional disturbance in the child should not be used to downplay the significance of adverse parental factors; assessment of the parent-infant/toddler relationship should be undertaken using standardised tools, as part of an integrated model of assessment (see Chapter Three).

> Highly skilled and long-term relationship-based practice that is underpinned by a clear logic model with regard to the mechanisms of change, and which targets recognised aetiological factors in terms of abusive parenting (see Chapter Four), should be used to bring about change in parenting, particularly in 'hard-to-reach' and 'resistant' families.

> Non-cooperation appears to be a significant factor in child deaths following abuse; it should be included as part of the assessment process and be the basis for compulsory intervention.

> Official measures of governance should focus on indicators of performance in relation to some of the methods of working highlighted here.

Training and recruitment

The report of the Social Work Task Force identifies the need for changes to the training of social workers (Social Work Task Force 2009). The findings of this review point to the need for the following changes in terms of recruitment, core training and continuing professional development:

i) Recruitment:

> Many of the failings of the child protection system have been attributed to the need for improved communication (Walker 2008), and the research highlights the importance of social workers being selected for training on the basis not only of educational qualifications, but also in terms of their personal qualities and development (see Chapter Four).

> Social work recruits should also be required to demonstrate a capacity to become fully reflective practitioners in terms of their ability to work towards gaining an understanding about their own attachment and relationship styles, and the implications for their practice.

ii) Basic training:

> Further changes to social work training are needed in terms of skills in relation to both assessment and intervention:

> > the application of clear theoretical and evidence-based models of: a) working in partnership with families; b) relationship-based methods of intervening; and c) structured clinical decision-making and assessment

> > the application of observational skills to interpret the parent-infant and parent-child relationship

> > an understanding of early child development and how to observe and interpret attachment problems, particularly those signifying disorganised attachment

> > methods of intervening to support families that are underpinned by and utilise the concepts from both attachment and psychodynamic methods of working.

iii) Continuing professional development:

> Upskilling of the existing workforce is urgently needed, and continuing professional development should be used to achieve this; training should focus explicitly on: a) skilled assessment of parent-infant and parent-child relationships using a range of standardised tools that improve observational skills; and b) partnership and relationship-based methods of working with families to bring about change.

> Social workers should have ongoing and regular opportunities to enhance their existing skills and to begin to utilise new and evidence-based methods of practice and working with families.

Integrated working

Transdisciplinary working should be adopted in which:

> members of different agencies work together jointly, sharing aims, information, tasks and responsibilities

> a lead worker, whose post is funded on a multiagency basis, plays a key role in designing and delivering a programme of unified care and co-ordinating services for the child and family

> one co-ordinated multiagency assessment is undertaken and used by all professionals

> families are included as partners (Sloper 2004)

> child psychotherapists and family therapists are core members of transdisciplinary teams (see Level 3, Figure 6.1) in keeping with the findings of this review and international research that highlights the range of specialist professionals who work as part of multidisciplinary teams in other countries.

There is a need for substantial development in Children's Trusts. The following have been highlighted at government level (adapted from the findings of Siraj-Blatchford and Siraj-Blatchford 2009; and Audit Commission 2008):

> an updated single source of future guidance comprising:

>> a clear vision of service integration to be disseminated and promoted to staff

>> a common definition of 'commissioning' for local government, the NHS and the police

>> clarification of the core objectives of the Every Child Matters policy to address the tension that some stakeholders see between the needs of families and children, and to make the roles of universal, targeted and preventative services clear

>> an overall (interdisciplinary) strategy for service assessment and intervention, which also provides a common language

>> agreement on service thresholds and tiers of need

>> consistent, cross-departmental support for local collaborative working between Children's Trusts, Local Strategic Partnerships and other thematic partnerships

> alignment of financial accounting and performance reporting frameworks to make it easier for local public bodies to understand one another's contributions and challenges and to align resources locally; the creation of opportunities for appropriate financial processes (aligning or pooling) as opposed to prescription

> better provision for workforce development, nationally and regionally, to support effective integrated delivery in the early years services

> more robust research that addresses the evidence gaps identified (further local research and development efforts should also be supported); the identification and promotion of agreed outcome measures and standardised research instruments

> procedures to enable the newly created Centre for Excellence and Outcomes in Children and Young People's Services to support Children's Trusts by benchmarking performance and sharing good practice.

Change by local councils and other local agencies should include:

> clarification of the objectives of integrated working for all those involved in service management and delivery

> development of an approach to service assessment and intervention that provides:

>> recognition of the additional burdens of integrated working in terms of, for example, the completion of CAF forms, duties of Lead Professional etc.

>> a common language and greater agreement on service thresholds and tiers of need

>> clarification about continued funding for service integration

>> engagement of the 'missing partners' in Children's Trusts, including voluntary sector organisations and families

>> the use of self-assessment questions to improve working (see Appendix B).

Training at all levels is needed to develop:

> leadership for integrated services

> a shared philosophy and vision

> better communication systems

> a clear staff review and supervision system

> shared understanding of roles

> training of service co-ordinators to ensure they have an adequate knowledge of the full range of services available in supporting the Every Child Matters agenda

> review of current governance and management arrangements for children's services to focus on delivering improved outcomes.

Workforce differentiation

> Greater differentiation of the social work workforce is required to enable them to develop new roles within community-based teams, particularly in schools and children's centres (see Level 1, Figure 6.1).

Continuity across the levels of service provision

> Practitioners at all levels are engaged in safeguarding work, and there is a need for better continuity across the different levels of service provision; the CAF should be promoted as a central mechanism linking the different levels of service provision.

> As suggested above, social workers should be part of transdisciplinary teams that are located at all service levels (see Figure 6.1 Levels 1 and 3).

Promoting the use of the CAF

> There is a need for further national guidance about the CAF and Lead Professional roles and processes, including a single nationally approved CAF form.

> The CAF offers a range of benefits for both service providers and users, but it is currently seriously underused; where the CAF is being used, the focus is often that of referral or a mechanism to get help, rather than as the beginning part of the helping process (Brandon et al. 2006).

> There is a need for further active implementation of the CAF across child welfare organisations, including schools. Strategic approaches are needed to plan, implement and review its introduction.

Other factors that enhance successful local implementation include:

> ensuring that practitioners have not only received multiagency and ongoing training in the use of the CAF and Lead Professional, but have also received training in partnership working that provides them with the skills not only to undertake a participatory assessment process, but also the necessary skills to undertake 'therapeutic' working with families

> case-based supervision for staff involved in undertaking assessment, if they are not routinely in receipt of supervision as part of their work

> workload allowances made for practitioners, so that workloads are reconfigured to allow for the increased demands made by this work, particularly in the short term

> ensuring that staff have access to appropriate IT systems

> ensuring that the responsibility and funding for Lead Professional work is shared across agencies

> assessment of all section 17 referrals from professionals in the first instance using the CAF.

Leadership

> New forms of leadership are needed for organisations with a multiprofessional workforce.

> Leaders are needed who can generate vision, new ways of working, innovative projects and responsive forms of organisational governance (Frost and Stein 2009).

At operational level

Models of working

A number of possible models of working have been highlighted (eg Thoburn 2009) and include:

> a 'team around the child and family' (eg Burton 2009; Siraj-Blatchford, Clarke, Needham 2007)

> a Social Work Unit comprising a qualified social worker, children's practitioner, unit co-ordinator and clinician time; the unit is headed by a consultant social worker (eg Reclaiming Social Work, Hackney)

> single worker with a very small caseload and 24-hour availability of supervision or consultation as, for example, in intensive family preservation models developed in the US that have been adapted for use in the UK (eg Tunstill et al 2009; Brandon and Connolly 2006)

> a co-working model derived from family therapy in which two workers share the Lead Professional role for the family as a whole (Thoburn 2009).

The emphasis of all models that are adopted, particularly within social care, should be on continuity in terms of the practitioner-client relationship eg the assessment process is the first stage of provision and should be undertaken by the same practitioner who will continue working with the family.

All models should have at least one member of the team who has specialist skills in terms of the provision of parent-infant/child psychotherapy and family therapy.

Safeguarding working environments

Findings from this research indicate that for holistic reflective practice to be facilitated, the interdependence of the practitioner, team and organisational contexts needs to be recognised (Ruch 2005). Practitioners need to work within safe containing contexts, characterised by:

> clear organisational and professional boundaries

> multifaceted reflective forums

> collaborative and communicative working practices

> open and 'contextually connected' managers

> containing, reflective spaces in which practitioners have the opportunity to think, feel and talk about their work with families.

Management

> Team structures and practices and team managers have a pivotal role in determining the existence and effectiveness of the type of reflective, containing spaces that have been highlighted throughout this document.

> Staff (including social workers) need permission from their employing organisations to make changes in their practices, and this in turn requires employing organisations to state clear goals in line with a child welfare orientation and develop holistic strategies to achieve these (Spratt 2001).

Supervision

The report of the Social Work Task Force identifies the need for clear national standards for the supervision of social work (Social Work Task Force 2009). Further changes are needed as follows:

> Key aspects of supervision should include support in undertaking the relationship-based aspects of supporting families and the provision of social and emotional support to staff; both have been shown to be positively related to beneficial outcomes for workers.

> It is not clear that either of the above tasks (in particular the latter) can be properly realised where the supervisory function is undertaken by the same person who provides case management; other methods of managing the tension between these two roles need to be found if the potential and important benefits of supervision are to be fully realised.

> Further resources should be devoted to training supervisors across all supervisory dimensions, and in particular those highlighted in Chapter Four.

Mapping of local need

> Local needs assessment should be undertaken to map the level of need within each local authority, and the services available to meet such need.

> Weighted tools (eg Corby 2003) should be used to monitor whether local decision-making is placing the right emphasis on safeguarding and support.

Organisational strategies for change

> The type of shifts in structure and in professional attitudes and practice that have been highlighted throughout this review can only be effectively implemented using formal organisational strategies for change.

> Organisational models should be used by managers to motivate staff to change by increasing the motivators for change while at the same time removing or decreasing the barriers, whether material, environmental or psychological; these should also address the role of ambivalence in the change process (Horwath and Morrison 2000).

At practitioner level

Practice

> The professional-client relationship should be made a pivotal part of all work with families across the safeguarding continuum.

> The development of relationship-based practice is dependent on practitioners and managers re-conceptualising their understanding of human behaviours - their own as well as those of the children and families they work with - and expanding the knowledge informing their practice.

> Practitioners should aim to provide: i) a supportive therapeutic stance based on principles of acceptance, empathy, genuineness and trust, all of which are essential to fostering a strong alliance between client and worker and to meeting some of the parents' unmet developmental needs (eg Luthar et al. 2007), particularly containment (see below); ii) a focus on interpersonal and relational issues aimed at providing parents with an opportunity to reflect on the parenting they are providing in the light of their own experiences of being parented, alongside the opportunity to increase their capacity for reflective functioning, and empathic parenting.

Assessment

> An integrated model of assessment should be used that combines actuarial risk assessment with the application of clinical skills and judgement alongside the use of evidence about what works and client preferences (see Chapter Three).

> Observation of parent-infant or parent-child interaction should comprise a core part of the assessment process, alongside an assessment of the child's socio-emotional functioning; such assessments should be undertaken using standardised assessment tools in conjunction with clinical skills.

> Practitioners should have access to the diverse range of standardised assessment tools that are now available, to use selectively as part of the assessment process.[1]

> Assessment should be undertaken by other specialists (eg parent-infant/child psychotherapists) if social workers do not have the necessary skill to undertake this themselves.[2]

Intervention

i) During the first four years of life:

> Intervention during pregnancy and the first three years of a child's life should be regarded as a priority and key to promoting the well-being of children.

> Early and intensive methods of support should be provided such as the Family Nurse Partnership programme.

> Support needs to be explicitly focused on bringing about change in parenting and in the parent-child relationship (ie in addition to addressing issues such as drug abuse, mental health problems or domestic violence); such change should be measured as part of the provision of intervention.

> Specialist dyadic interventions such as parent-infant/toddler/child psychotherapy should be used to address early relationship problems.

> Manualised programmes should be offered to high-risk parents/families, as part of a broader relationship-based approach to intervening with such families.

ii) With children over four years of age:

> Support, once again, needs to be explicitly focused on bringing about change in parenting and in the parent-child relationship (ie in addition to addressing issues such as drug abuse, mental health problems or domestic violence); and such change should be assessed as part of the provision of intervention.

> Parenting skills should be addressed using manualised evidence-based programmes alongside the provision of relationship-based social work interventions.

> Children who have been exposed to seriously inadequate parenting environments and who show signs of emotional disturbance including disorganised attachment, should be provided with access to therapeutic services (eg child psychotherapy) that are focused on improving the child's emotional functioning and their capacity for trusting relationships.

1. For a comprehensive overview of standardised instruments see, for example, Austin (2009).

2. CPD provides key opportunities for social workers to acquire additional specialist skills in the assessment of parent-infant/child interaction using standardised tools.

References

Alexander C and Charles G (2009) 'Caring, Mutuality and Reciprocity in Social Worker-Client Relationships' *Journal of Social Work* 9 (1) 5-22

Anning A, Cottrell DM, Frost N, Green J and Robinson M (2006) *Developing Multiprofessional Teamwork for Integrated Children's Services*. Maidenhead: Open University Press

Asquith S, Clark C and Waterhouse L (2005) *The Role of the Social Worker in the 21st Century: A literature review*. Edinburgh: Scottish Executive

Audit Commission (2008) *Are We There Yet? Improving governance and resource management in children's trusts*. London: Audit Commission

Austin MJ (2009) *Evidence for Child Welfare Practice*. London: Routledge

Azar ST, Lauretti AF and Loding BV (1998) 'The Evaluation of Parental Fitness in Termination of Parental Rights Cases: A functional-contextual perspective' *Clinical Child and Family Psychology Review* 1 (2) 77-100

Bain K (2009) 'Modernising Children's Services: Partnership and participation in policy and practice' in Harris J and White V (eds) *Modernising Social Work: Critical considerations*. Bristol: The Policy Press

Bakermans-Kranenburg MJ, van IJzendoorn MH and Juffer F (2003) 'Less is More: Meta-analyses of sensitivity and attachment interventions in early childhood' *Psychological Bulletin* 129 (2) 195-215

Barlow J, Johnston I, Kendrick D, Polnay L and Stewart-Brown S (2006) 'Individual and Group-based Parenting Programmes for the Treatment of Physical Child Abuse and Neglect' *Cochrane Database of Systematic Reviews* (3) Article no: CD005463

Barlow J and Schrader McMillan A (2010) *Safeguarding Children from Emotional Maltreatment*. London: Jessica Kingsley Publishers

Barlow J and Svanberg PO (eds) (2009) *Keeping the Baby in Mind: Infant mental health in practice*. London: Routledge

Barlow J and Underdown A (2008) 'Supporting Parenting During Infancy', in Jackson C, Hill K and Lavis P (eds) *Child and Adolescent Mental Health Today: A handbook*. London: Mental Health Foundation

Bateman A and Fonagy P (2004) *Psychotherapy for Borderline Personality Disorder: Mentalization-based treatment*. New York: Oxford University Press

Beebe B and Lachmann FM (1987) 'Mother-Infant Mutual Influence and Precursors of Psychic Structure' in Goldberg A (ed) Progress in *Self Psychology, volume 3*. London: Routledge

Beebe B and Lachmann FM (2005) *Infant Research and Adult Treatment: Co-constructing interactions*. London: Routledge

Belsky J (1993) 'Etiology of Child Maltreatment: A developmental-ecological analysis' *Psychological Bulletin* 114 (3) 413-434

Belt R and Punamaki RL (2007) 'Mother-Infant Group Psychotherapy as an Intensive Treatment in Early Interaction Among Mothers with Substance Abuse Problems' *Journal of Child Psychotherapy* 33 (2) 202-220

Bion WR (1967) *Second Thoughts*. London: William Heinemann

Bion WR (1970) *Attention and Interpretation*. London: Tavistock Publications

Boddy J and Statham J (2009) *European Perspectives on Social Work: Models of education and professional roles*. London: Thomas Coram Research Unit, Institute of Education

Boyd E (2007) 'Commentary: Containing the container' *Journal of Social Work Practice* 21 (2) 203-206

Brandell JR and Ringel S (2004) 'Psychodynamic Perspectives on Relationship: Implications of new findings from human attachment and the neurosciences for social work education' *Families in Society: The Journal of Contemporary Human Services* 85 (4) 549-556

Brandon M, Belderson P, Warren C, Gardner R, Howe D, Dodsworth J and Black J (2008) 'The Preoccupation with Thresholds in Cases of Child Death or Serious Injury through Abuse and Neglect' *Child Abuse Review* 17 (5) 313-330

Brandon M and Connolly J (2006) 'Are Intensive Preservation Services Useful? A UK study' *Journal of Family Preservation* 9 56-69

Brandon M, Howe A, Dagley V, Salter C and Warren C (2006) 'What Appears to be Helping or Hindering Practitioners in Implementing the Common Assessment Framework and Lead Professionals Working?' *Child Abuse Review* 15 (6) 396-413

Brandon M and Thoburn J (2008) 'Safeguarding Children in the UK: A longitudinal study of services to children suffering or likely to suffer significant harm' *Child and Family Social Work* 13 (4) 365-377

Braun D, Davis H and Mansfield P (2006) *How Helping Works: Towards a shared model of process.* London: Parentline Plus

Browne K (1995) 'Predicting maltreatment' in Reder P and Lucey C (eds) *Assessment of Parenting: Psychiatric and psychological contributions.* London: Routledge

Burton S (2009) *The Oversight and Review of Cases in the Light of Changing Circumstances and New Information: How do people respond to new (and challenging) information?* London: C4EO

Cabinet Office (2007) *Reaching Out: Think family.* London: Cabinet Office

Cicchetti D and Carlson V (eds) (1989) *Child Maltreatment: Theory and research on the causes and consequences of child abuse and neglect.* Cambridge: CUP

Cicchetti D and Lynch M (1993) 'Toward an Ecological/Transactional Model of Community Violence and Child Maltreatment: Consequences for children's development' *Psychiatry* 56 (1) 96-118

Cicchetti D and Rizley R (1981) 'Developmental Perspectives on the Etiology, Intergenerational Transmission, and Sequelae of Child Maltreatment' *New Directions for Child Development* 1981 (11) 31-55

Cicchetti D, Toth SL, Bush MA and Gillespie JF (1988) 'Stage-Salient Issues: A transactional model of intervention' *New Directions for Child and Adolescent Development* 1988 (39) 123–145

Cleaver H and Walker S (2004) 'From Policy to Practice: The implementation of a new framework for social work assessments of children and families' *Child and Family Social Work* 9 (1) 81-90

Cohen NJ, Lojkasek M, Muir E, Muir R and Parker CJ (2002) 'Six-Month Follow-Up of Two Mother-Infant Psychotherapies' *Infant Mental Health Journal* 23 (4) 361-380

Cohen NJ, Muir E, Lojkasek M, Muir R, Parker CJ, Barwick M and Brown M (1999) 'Watch, Wait and Wonder: Testing the effectiveness of a new approach to mother-infant psychotherapy' *Infant Mental Health Journal* 20 (4) 429-451

Colton MJ, Drury C and Williams M (1995) *Children in Need: Family Support under the Children Act 1989.* Aldershot: Avebury

Committee on the Rights of the Child (1989) *The United Nations Convention on the Rights of the Child*. UNICEF

Connolly M (2007) 'Practice Frameworks: Conceptual maps to guide interventions in child welfare' *British Journal of Social Work* 37 (5) 825-837

Cooper A, Hetherington R and Katz I (2003) *The Risk Factor: Child protection system work for children*. London: Demos

Cooper A and Lousada J (2005) *Borderline Welfare: Feeling and fear of feeling in modern welfare*. London: Karnac Books

Corby B (2003) 'Supporting Families and Protecting Children' *Journal of Social Work* 3 (2) 195-210

Corby B, Millar M and Pope A (2002) 'Assessing Children in Need Assessments: A parental perspective' *Practice* 14 (4) 5-15

Cornell T and Hamrin V (2008) 'Clinical Interventions for Children with Attachment Problems' *Journal of Child and Adolescent Psychiatric Nursing* 21 (1) 35-47

Coveney P and Highfield R (1996) *Frontiers of Complexity: The search for order in a chaotic world*. New York: Ballantine Books

Cowan P and Cowan CP (2008) 'Diverging family Policies to Promote Children's Well-being in the UK and US: Some relevant data from family research and intervention studies' *Journal of Children's Services* 3 (4) 4-16

Cramer B and Stern DN (1988) 'Evaluation of Changes in Mother-Infant Brief Psychotherapy: A single case study' *Infant Mental Health Journal* 9 (1) 20-45

Crawshaw M (2008) 'What is Reflective Practice?' York: Department of Social Policy and Social Work, University of York Available online at: www.york.ac.uk/depts/spsw/ documents/ Day4HandoutWhatisreflectivepractice.doc (accessed April 2010)

Crittenden PM (1981) 'Abusing, Neglecting, Problematic, and Adequate Dyads: Differentiating by patterns of interaction' *Merrill-Palmer Quarterly* 27 (3) 201-218

Davis H (2009) 'The Family Partnership Model: Understanding the processes of prevention and early intervention' in Barlow J and Svanberg PO (2009) op. cit.

Davis H and Day C (2010) *Working in Partnership: The Family Partnership Model*. London: Pearson Assessment

Davis H, Day C and Bidmead C (2002) *Working in Partnership with Parents: The Parent Adviser Model*. London: Harcourt Assessment

Department for Children, Schools and Families (2007a) *Children's Plan: Building brighter futures*. London: The Stationery Office (Cm 7280)

Department for Children, Schools and Families (2007b) *Effective Integrated Working: Findings of Concept of Operations Study*. London: Department for Children, Schools and Families

Department for Children, Schools and Families (2009) *The Protection of Children in England: Action plan*. London: The Stationery Office (Cm 7589)

Department for Children, Schools and Families (2010) *Working Together to Safeguard Children: A guide to inter-agency working to safeguard and promote the welfare of children*. London: Department for Children, Schools and Families

Department for Children, Schools and Families, Department of Health and Department for Business, Innovation and Skills, with the Social Work Reform Board (2010) *Building a Safe and Confident Future: Implementing the recommendations of the Social Work Task Force*. London: Department for Children, Schools and Families

Department for Education and Skills (2003) *Every Child Matters*. London: The Stationery Office (Cm 5860)

Department for Education and Skills (2004) *Every Child Matters: Change for children*. London: Department for Education and Skills

Department for Education and Skills (2006) *Working Together to Safeguard Children: A guide to inter-agency working to safeguard and promote the welfare of children*. London: The Stationery Office

Department for Education and Skills, Department of Health and Home Office (2003) *Keeping Children Safe: The government's response to the Victoria Climbié Inquiry Report and Joint Chief Inspectors' report Safeguarding Children*. London: The Stationery Office (Cm 5861)

Department of Health (1995) *Child Protection: Messages from research*. London: Department of Health

Department of Health (1998) *Modernising Social Services: Promoting independence, improving protection, raising standards*. London: The Stationery Office (Cm 4169)

Department of Health (2000) *Framework for the Assessment of Children in Need and their Families*. London: Department of Health

Department of Health and Department for Children, Schools and Families (2008) *Child Health Promotion Programme: Pregnancy and the first five years of life*. London: Department of Health

Department of Health, Home Office and Department for Education and Employment (1999) *Working Together to Safeguard Children*. London: Department of Health

DiLillo D, Perry AR and Fortier M (2005) 'Child Physical Abuse and Neglect' in Hersen M and Thomas JC (eds) *Comprehensive Handbook of Personality and Psychopathology: Volume 3, child psychopathology*. Hoboken, NJ: John Wiley & Sons

Donald T and Jureidini J (2004) 'Parenting Capacity' *Child Abuse Review* 13 (1) 5-17

Dorsey S, Mustillo SA, Farmer EMZ and Elbogen E (2008) 'Caseworker Assessments of Risk for Recurrent Maltreatment: Association with case-specific risk factors and re-reports' *Child Abuse & Neglect* 32 (3) 377-391

Dretzke J, Davenport C, Frew E, Barlow J, Stewart-Brown S, Bayliss S, Taylor RS, Sandercock J and Hyde C (2009) 'The Clinical Effectiveness of Different Parenting Programmes for Children with Conduct Problems: A systematic review of randomised controlled trials' *Child and Adolescent Psychiatry and Mental Health* 3 (7)

Easton C, Morris M and Gee G (2010) LARC2: *Integrated Children's Services and the CAF Process*. Slough: NfER

Evans T (2009) 'Managing to be Professional? Team managers and practitioners in modernised social work' in Harris J and White V (eds) *Modernising Social Work*. Bristol: Policy Press

Farmer E and Owen M (1995) *Child Protection Practice: Private risks and public remedies*. London: The Stationery Office

Fauth R, Jelicic H, Hart D, Burton S, Shemmings D, Bergeron C, White K and Morris M (2010) *Effective Practice to Protect Children Living in 'Highly Resistant' Families*. London: C4EO

Flaskas C (2007) 'Systemic and Psychoanalytic Ideas: Using knowledge in social work' *Journal of Social Work Practice* 21 (2) 131-147

Fonagy P (1999) 'Transgenerational Consistencies of Attachment: A new theory.' (Paper to the Developmental and Psychoanalytic Discussion Group, American Psychoanalytic Association Meeting, Washington DC 13 May 1999.) Available online at: www.dspp.com/papers/fonagy2.htm (accessed April 2010)

Fonagy P, Target M, Gergely G, Allen JG and Bateman AW (2003) 'The Developmental Roots of Borderline Personality Disorder in Early Attachment Relationships: A theory and some evidence' *Psychoanalytic Inquiry* 23 (3) 412-459

Freedberg S (2008) *Relational Theory for Social Work Practice: A feminist perspective.* New York and London: Routledge

Frost N and Stein M (2009) 'Editorial: Outcomes of integrated working with children and young people' *Children and Society* 23 (5) 315-319

Garrett PM (2009) *'Transforming' Children's Services? Social Work, Neoliberalism and the 'Modern' World.* Maidenhead: Open University Press

Gerhardt S (2004) *Why Love Matters: How affection shapes a baby's brain.* London: Routledge

Gibbons J (1995) *The Child Protection System: Objectives and evaluation.* University of East Anglia/Lancaster University

Gilbert R, Kemp A, Thoburn J, Sidebotham P, Radford L, Glaser D and MacMillan HL (2009a) 'Recognising and Responding to Child Maltreatment' *The Lancet* 373 (9658) 167-180

Gilbert R, Spatz Widom C, Browne K, Fergusson D, Webb E and Janson S (2009b) 'Burden and Consequences of Child Maltreatment in High-Income Countries' *The Lancet* 373 (9657) 68-81

Giller H, Gormley C and Williams P (1992) *The Effectiveness of Child Protection Procedures: An evaluation of child protection procedures in four A.C.P.C. areas.* Knutsford: Social Information Systems

Gilligan P and Manby M (2008) 'The Common Assessment Framework: Does the reality match the rhetoric?' *Child and Family Social Work* 13 (2) 177-187

Gray J (2001) 'The Framework for the Assessment of Children in Need and their Families' *Child Psychology and Psychiatry Review* 6 (1) 4-10

Gray M, Plath D and Webb SA (2009) *Evidenced-Based Social Work: A critical stance.* London: Routledge

Hardy F and Darlington Y (2008) 'What Parents Value from Formal Support Services in the Context of Identified Child Abuse' *Child and Family Social Work* 13 (3) 252-261

Harnett P (2007) 'A Procedure for Assessing Parents' Capacity for Change in Child Protection Cases' *Children and Youth Services Review* 29 (9) 1179-1188

Harnett P and Dawe S (2008) 'Reducing Child Abuse Potential in Families Identified by Social Services: Implications for assessment and treatment' *Brief Treatment and Crisis Intervention* 8 (3) 226-235

Harnett P and Day C (2008) 'Developing Pathways to Assist Parents to Exit the Child Protection System in Australia' *Clinical Psychologist* 12 (3) 79-95

Harris J (2009) 'Customer-Citizenship in Modernised Social Work' in Harris J and White V (eds) *Modernising Social Work: Critical considerations.* Bristol: The Policy Press

Hayes D and Spratt T (2009) 'Child Welfare Interventions: Patterns of social work practice' *British Journal of Social Work* 39 (8) 1575-1597

Haynes RB, Devereaux PJ and Guyatt GH (2002) Physicians' and Patients' Choices in Evidence Based Practice: Evidence does not make decisions, people do' *British Medical Journal* 324 (7350) 1350

Hicks L and Stein M (2010) *Neglect Matters: A multi-agency guide for professionals working together on behalf of teenagers*. London: Department for Children, Schools and Families

Hingley-Jones H and Mandin P (2007) 'Getting to the Root of Problems: The role of systemic ideas in helping social work students to develop relationship-based practice' *Journal of Social Work Practice* 21 (2) 177-191

Horwath J and Morrison T (2000) 'Identifying and Implementing Pathways for Organizational Change – Using the Framework for the Assessment of Children in Need and their Families as a case example' *Child and Family Social Work* 5 (3) 245-254

Horwath J and Morrison T (2007) 'Collaboration, Integration and Change in Children's Services: Critical issues and key ingredients' *Child Abuse & Neglect* 31 (1) 55-69

Houston S (2001) 'Beyond Social Constructionism: Critical realism and social work' *British Journal of Social Work* 31 (6) 845-861

Howe D (1997) 'Psychosocial and Relationship-Based Theories for Child and Family Social Work: Political philosophy, psychology and welfare practice' *Child and Family Social Work* 2 (3) 161-169

Howe D (1998) 'Relationship-Based Thinking and Practice in Social Work' *Journal of Social Work Practice* 12 (1) 45-56

Howe D (2005) *Child Abuse and Neglect: Attachment, development and intervention*. Basingstoke: Palgrave Macmillan

Howe D (submitted) 'The Safety of Children and the Parent-Worker Relationship in Cases of Child Abuse and Neglect' *Child Abuse Review*

Howe D, Brandon M, Hinings D and Schofield G (1999) *Attachment Theory, Child Maltreatment and Family Support: A practice and assessment model*. Basingstoke: Palgrave Macmillan

Jack R (2005) 'Strengths-Based Practice in Statutory Care and Protection Work' in Nash M, Munford R and O'Donoghue K (eds) *Social Work Theories in Action*. London: Jessica Kingsley

Joint Chief Inspectors (2002) *Safeguarding Children: A joint chief inspectors' report on arrangements to safeguard children*. London: Department of Health

Joint Chief Inspectors (2005) *Safeguarding Children: The second joint chief inspectors' report on arrangements to safeguard children*. London: Commission for Social Care Inspection

Katz I and Hetherington R (2006) 'Cooperating and Communicating: A European perspective on integrating services for children' *Child Abuse Review* 15 (6) 429-439

Keatinge D, Fowler C and Briggs C (2008) 'Evaluating the Family Partnership Model (FPM) program and implementation in practice in New South Wales, Australia' *Australian Journal of Advanced Nursing* 25 (2) 28-35

Kelly GA (1991) *The Psychology of Personal Constructs. Volume One: Theory and personality*. London: Routledge

Keren M, Feldman R and Tyano S (2001) 'Diagnosis and Interactive Patterns of Infants Refereed to a Community-Based Infant Mental Health Clinic' *Journal of the American Academy of Child and Adolescent Psychiatry* 40 (1) 27-35

Knei-Paz C (2009) 'The Central Role of the Therapeutic Bond in a Social Agency Setting: Clients' and social workers' perceptions' *Journal of Social Work* 9 (2) 178-198

Laming H (2003) *The Victoria Climbié Inquiry. Report of an Inquiry.* London: The Stationery Office (CM5730)

Laming H (2009) *The Protection of Children in England: A progress report.* London: The Stationery Office (HC 330)

Larzelere RE and Patterson GR (1990) 'Parental Management: Mediator of the effect of socioeconomic status on early delinquency' *Criminology* 28 (2) 301-324

Leventhal H, Lambert JF, Diefenbach M and Leventhal EA (1997) 'From Compliance to Social-Self-Regulation: Models of the compliance process' in Blackwell B (eds) *Treatment Compliance and the Therapeutic Alliance.* Amsterdam: Harwood Academic Publishers

Lewin R (1999) *Complexity: Life at the Edge of Chaos.* Chicago: The University of Chicago Press

Lieberman AF (1999) 'Negative Maternal Attributions: Effects on toddlers' sense of self' *Psychoanalytic Enquiry* 19 (5) 737-756

Lissack MR (1996) 'Chaos and Complexity - Knowledge management?' Available online at: www.leadervalues.com/Content/detail.asp?ContentDetailID=47 (accessed April 2010)

Littell JH and Girvin H (2005) 'Caregivers' Readiness for Change: Predictive validity in a child welfare sample' *Child Abuse & Neglect* 29 (1) 59-80

Littell JH and Girvin H (2006) 'Correlates of Problem Recognition and Intentions to Change Among Caregivers of Abused and Neglected Children' *Child Abuse & Neglect* 30 (12) 1381-1399

Lonne B, Parton N, Thomson J and Harries M (2008) *Reforming Child Protection.* Abingdon: Routledge

Lord P, Kinder K, Wilkin A, Atkinson M and Harland J (2008) *Evaluating the Early Impact of Integrated Children's Services: Round 1 summary report.* Slough: NfER

Lorgelly P, Bachmann M, Shreeve A, Reading R, Thoburn J, Mugford M, O'Brien M and Husbands C (2009) 'Is it Feasible to Pool Funds for Local Children's Services in England? Evidence from the National Evaluation of Children's Trust Pathfinders' *Journal of Health Services Research & Policy* 14 (1) 27-34

Luthar SS, Suchman NE and Altomare M (2007) 'Relational Psychotherapy Mothers' Group: A randomized clinical trial for substance abusing mothers' *Development and Psychopathology* 19 (1) 243-261

Lyons-Ruth K (1996) 'Attachment Relationships Among Children with Aggressive Behavior Problems: The role of disorganized early attachment patterns' *Journal of Consulting and Clinical Psychology* 64 (1) 64-73

McAuley C and Cleaver D (2006) Improving Service Delivery – *Introducing Outcomes-Based Accountability.* London: IDeA

MacMillan HL, Wathen CN, Barlow J, Fergusson DM, Levanthal JM and Taussig HN (2009) 'Interventions to Prevent Child Maltreatment and Associated Impairment' *The Lancet* 373 (9659) 250-266

Mandin P (2007) 'The Contribution of Systems and Object-Relation Theories to an Understanding of the Therapeutic Relationship in Social Work Practice' *Journal of Social Work Practice* 21 (2) 149-162

Mason C, May-Chahal C, Regan S and Thorpe D (2005) 'Differentiating Common Assessment Cases from other types of Cases: The research evidence for CAF responses' Lancaster University Available online at: www.lums.lancs.ac.uk/files/ccips/7115/download (accessed April 2010)

May-Chahal C and Cawson P (2005) 'Measuring Child Maltreatment in the United Kingdom: A study of the prevalence of child abuse and neglect' *Child Abuse & Neglect* 29 (9) 969–984

Menzies-Lyth IEP (1960) 'A Case Study in the Functioning of Social Systems as a Defence against Anxiety' *Human Relations* 13 (2) 95-121

Millar M and Corby B (2006) 'The Framework for the Assessment of Children in Need and their Families – A Basis for a 'Therapeutic' Encounter?' *British Journal of Social Work* 36 (6) 887-899

Montgomery P, Gardner F, Bjornstad G and Ramchandani P (2009) *Systematic Reviews of Interventions Following Physical Abuse: Helping practitioners and expert witnesses improve the outcomes of child abuse – summary.* London: Department for Children, Schools and Families

Munro E (2005) 'What Tools Do We Need to Improve Identification of Child Abuse?' *Child Abuse Review* 14 (6) 374-388

O'Brien M, Bachmann MO, Jones NR, Reading R, Thoburn J, Husbands C, Shreeve A and Watson J (2009) 'Do Integrated Children's Services Improve Children's Outcomes?: Evidence from England's children's trust pathfinders' *Children and Society* 23 (5) 320-335

OXPIP (2005) *Oxford Parent Infant Project Report on Assessment Procedures.* Oxford: OXPIP

Page T and Norwood R (2007) 'Attachment Theory and the Social Work Curriculum' *Advances in Social Work* 8 (1) 30-48

Pawson R and Tilley N (1997) *Realistic Evaluation.* London: Sage

Payne M (2008) 'Complexity and Social Work Theory and Practice' *Social Work Now* 39 (April) 15-20

Peckover S, Hall C and White S (2009) 'From Policy to Practice: The implementation and negotiation of technologies in everyday child welfare' *Children and Society* 23 (2) 136-148

Percy-Smith J (2006) 'What Works in Strategic Partnerships for Children: A research review' *Children and Society* 20 (4) 313-323

Perry BD (2002) 'Childhood Experience and the Expression of Genetic Potential: What childhood neglect tells us about nature and nurture' *Brain and Mind* 3 (1) 79-100

Peters R and Barlow J (2003) 'Systematic Review of Instruments Designed to Predict Child Maltreatment During the Antenatal and Postnatal Periods' *Child Abuse Review* 12 (6) 416-439

Petr CG (ed) (2009) *Multidimensional Evidenced-Based Practice: Synthesizing knowledge, research and values.* Abingdon: Routledge

Pithouse A (2006) 'A Common Assessment for Children in Need? Mixed messages from a pilot study in Wales' *Child Care in Practice* 12 (3) 199-217

Pithouse A, Hall C, Peckover S and White S (2009) 'A Tale of Two CAFs: The impact of the electronic common assessment framework' *British Journal of Social Work* 39 (4) 599-612

Platt D (2001) 'Refocusing Children's Services: Evaluation of an initial assessment process' *Child and Family Social Work* 6 (2) 139-148

Platt D (2006a) 'Investigation or Initial Assessment of Child Concerns? The impact of the refocusing initiative on social work practice' *British Journal of Social Work* 36 (2) 267-281

Platt D (2006b) 'Threshold Decisions: How social workers prioritize referrals of child concern' *Child Abuse Review* 15 (1) 4-18

Platt D (2008) 'Care or Control? The effects of investigations and initial assessments on the social worker-parent relationship' *Journal of Social Work Practice* 22 (3) 301-315

Prinz RJ, Sanders MR, Shapiro CJ, Whitaker DJ and Lutzker JR (2009) 'Population-based Prevention of Child Maltreatment: The US triple P system population trial' *Prevention Science* 10 (1) 1-12

Pritchard C and Williams R (2009) 'Comparing Possible 'Child-Abuse-Related-Deaths' in England and Wales with the Major Developed Countries 1974–2006: Signs of Progress?' *British Journal of Social Work* Advance access: doi: 10.1093/bjsw/bcp089

Prochaska JO and DiClemente CC (1982) 'Transtheoretical Therapy: Toward a more integrative model of change' *Psychotherapy: Theory, Research and Practice* 19 (3) 276-288

Renn P (2009) 'Infant Observation and Adult Psychotherapy: How developmental studies are informing clinical work with adults' Available online at: www.counselling-directory.org.uk/counselloradvice10026.html (accessed April 2010)

Robinson M, Atkinson M and Downing D (2008a) *Integrated Children's Services: Enablers, challenges and impact.* Slough: NfER

Robinson M, Atkinson M and Downing D (2008b) *Supporting Theory Building in Integrated Services Research.* Slough: NfER

Rogers CR (1957) 'The Necessary and Sufficient Conditions of Therapeutic Personality Change' *Journal of Consulting Clinical Psychology* 21 (2) 95-103

Rogers CR (1959) 'A Theory of Therapy, Personality and Interpersonal Relationships as Developed in the Client-Centered Framework' in Koch S (ed) *Psychology: A study of a science, vol III: Formulations of the person and the social context.* New York: McGraw Hill

Rowe A (2009) 'Perinatal home visiting: Implementing the Nurse–Family Partnership in England' in Barlow J and Svanberg PO (2009) op. cit.

Rowlands J (2009) 'Does Complexity Theory Offer Anything to the Understanding of Children in Need?' *Journal of Children's Services* 4 (2) 25-35

Ruch G (2005) 'Relationship-Based Practice and Reflective Practice: Holistic approaches to contemporary child care social work' *Child and Family Social Work* 10 (2) 111-123

Rutter M, Kreppner J and Sonuga-Barke E (2009) 'Emanuel Miller Lecture: Attachment insecurity, disinhibited attachment, and attachment disorders: where do research findings leave the concepts?' *Journal of Child Psychology and Psychiatry* 50 (5) 529-543

Sable P (1996) 'Attachment Theory and Social Work Education' *Journal of Teaching in Social Work* 12 (1 & 2) 19-38

Saleebey D (1996) 'The Strengths Perspective in Social Work Practice: Extensions and cautions' *Social Work* 41 (3) 296-305

Sanders MR, Pidgeon AM, Gravestock F, Connors MD, Brown S and Young RW (2004) 'Does Parental Attributional Retraining and Anger Management Enhance the Effects of the Triple P-Positive Parenting Program with Parents at Risk of Child Maltreatment?' *Behavior Therapy* 35 (3) 513-535

Schore AN (1994) *Affect Regulation and the Origin of the Self: The neurobiology of emotional development.* Hillsdale NJ: Lawrence Erlbaum Associates, Inc

Scottish Executive (2002) *'It's everyone's job to make sure I'm alright' Report of the Child Protection Audit and Review.* Edinburgh: Scottish Executive

Scottish Executive (2006) *Changing Lives: Report of the 21st century social work review.* Scotland: Scottish Executive

Scourfield J and Pithouse A (2006) 'Lay and Professional Knowledge in Social Work: Reflections from ethnographic research on child protection' *European Journal of Social Work* 9 (3) 323-337

Shlonsky A and Wagner D (2005) 'The Next Step: Integrating actuarial risk assessment and clinical judgment into an evidence-based practice framework in CPS case management' *Children and Youth Services Review* 27 (4) 409-427

Siraj-Blatchford I, Clarke K and Needham M (2007) *The Team Around the Child: Multi-agency working in the early years.* Stoke-on-Trent: Trentham Books

Siraj-Blatchford I and Siraj-Blatchford J (2009) *Improving Development Outcomes for Children through Effective Practice in Integrating Early Years Services.* London: C4EO

Slade A, Sadler L, de Dios-Kenn C, Webb D, Currier-Ezepchick J and Mayes, L (2005) 'Minding the Baby: A Reflective Parenting Program' in King RA, Neubauer PB, Abrams S and Dowling AS (eds) *The Psychoanalytic Study of the Child Vol 60* New Haven: Yale University Press

Sloper P (2004) 'Facilitators and Barriers for Co-Ordinated Multi-Agency Services' *Child: Care, Health and Development* 30 (6) 571-580

Smith C and White S (1997) 'Parton, Howe and Postmodernity: A critical comment on mistaken identity' *British Journal of Social Work* 27 (2) 275-295

Social Services Inspectorate (1997) *Messages from Inspections: Child protection inspections* 1992-1996. London: DH

Social Work Task Force (2009) *Building a safe, confident future: the final report of the Social Work Task Force.* London: Department for Children, Schools and Families

Sousa L and Eusebio C (2007) 'When Multi-Problem Poor Individuals' Myths Meet Social Services Myths' *Journal of Social Work* 7 (2) 217-237

Spratt T (2001) 'The Influence of Child Protection Orientation on Child Welfare Practice' *British Journal of Social Work* 31 (6) 933-954

Spratt T and Callan J (2004) 'Parents' Views on Social Work Interventions in Child Welfare Cases' *British Journal of Social Work* 34 (2) 199-224

Sroufe LA (1995) *Emotional Development: The organization of emotional life in the early years.* Cambridge: Cambridge University Press

Sroufe LA (2005) 'Attachment and Development: A prospective, longitudinal study from birth to adulthood' *Attachment & Human Development* 7 (4) 349-367

Steele H and Siever P (2010) 'An Attachment Perspective on Borderline Personality Disorder: Advances in gene–environment considerations' *Current Psychiatry Reports* 12 (1) 61-67

Stepney P (2006) 'Mission Impossible? Critical practice in social work' *British Journal of Social Work* 36 (8) 1289-1307

Stern D (1998) *The Interpersonal World of the Infant: A view from psychoanalysis and development.* London: Karnac Books

Stevens I and Cox P (2008) 'Complexity Theory: Developing new understandings of child protection in field settings and in residential child care' *British Journal of Social Work* 38 (7) 1320-1336

Stevens I and Hassett P (2007) 'Applying Complexity Theory to Risk in Child Protection Practice' *Childhood* 14 (1) 128-144

Sudbery J (2002) 'Key Features of Therapeutic Social Work: The use of relationship' *Journal of Social Work Practice* 16 (2) 149-162

Tarabulsy GM, Pascuzzo K, Moss E, St-Laurent D, Bernier A, Cyr C and Dubois-Comtois K (2008) 'Attachment-Based Intervention for Maltreating Families' *American Journal of Orthopsychiatry* 78 (3) 322-332

Thoburn J and members of the Making Research Count Consortium (2009) *Effective Interventions for Complex Families where there are Concerns about, or Evidence of, a Child Suffering Significant Harm.* London: C4EO

Thompson S and Thompson N (2008) *The Critically Reflective Practitioner.* Basingstoke: Palgrave Macmillan

Thorpe D, Regan S, Mason C and May-Chahal C (2007) 'Making a Case for Common Assessment Framework Responses to Concerns about Children' *Social Work and Social Sciences Review* 12 (3) 40-56

Toasland J (2007) 'Containing the Container: An exploration of the containing role of management in a social work context' *Journal of Social Work Practice* 21 (2) 197-202

Toth SL, Maughan A, Todd Manly J, Spagnola M and Cicchetti D (2002) 'The Relative Efficacy of Two Interventions in Altering Maltreated Preschool Children's Representational Models: Implications for attachment theory' *Development and Psychopathology* 14 (4) 877-908

Tunstill J and Aldgate J (2000) *Services for Children in Need: From policy to practice.* London: The Stationery Office

Tunstill J, Blewett J and Meadows P (2009) *An Evaluation of the Delivery of Targeted Family Support by Action for Children.* London: Synergy Research and Consulting Ltd .

Utting D, Monteiro H and Ghate D (2007) *Interventions for Children at Risk of Developing Antisocial Personality Disorder.* London: Policy Research Bureau

Utting D, Rose W and Pugh G (2001) *Better Results for Children and Families: Involving communities in planning services based on outcomes.* London: NCVCCO

van IJzendoorn MH, Schuengel C and Bakermans-Kranenberg J (1999) 'Disorganized Attachment in Early Childhood: Meta-analysis of precursors, concomitants and sequelae' *Development and Psychopathology* 11 (2) 225-250

Wahab S (2005) 'Motivational Interviewing and Social Work Practice' *Journal of Social Work* 5 (1) 45-60

Walker J (2008) 'Communication and Social Work from an Attachment Perspective' *Journal of Social Work Practice* 22 (1) 5-13

Walsh F (2008) 'Using Theory to Support a Family Resilience Framework in Practice' *Social Work Now* 39 (April) 5-14

Ward H, Smith N, Garnett L, Booth A and Everett G (2002) *Evaluation of the Introduction of Inter-Agency Referral Documentation (Children in Need and in Need of Assessment Consent Form) in North East Lincolnshire.* Loughborough: Centre for Child and Family Research, Loughborough University Available online at: www.lboro.ac.uk/research/ccfr/Publications/Interagencyreferral.pdf (accessed April 2010)

Wattam C (1992) *Making a Case in Child Protection*. Harlow: Longman

White S, Hall C and Peckover S (2009) 'The Descriptive Tyranny of the Common Assessment Framework: Technologies of Categorization and Professional Practice in Child Welfare' *British Journal of Social Work* 39 (7) 1197-1217

White A and Walsh P (2006) *Risk Assessment in Child Welfare: An issues paper*. Ashfield: NSW Department of Community Services

Woodcock J (2003) 'The Social Work Assessment of Parenting: An exploration' *British Journal of Social Work* 33 (1) 87-106

Worrall-Davies A and Cottrell D (2009) 'Outcome Research and Interagency Work with Children: What does it tell us about what the CAMHS contribution should look like?' *Children and Society* 23 (5) 336-346

Appendix A

Method

Search aims

A limited search was undertaken to identify national and international studies and theoretical papers published in English from 2000-2009 in the following areas:

> papers that described or explored the organisational issues or challenges for those working within child protection; this included organisational working arrangements, operational frameworks, ways of working, tools

> papers that described or explored the issues or challenges of working with families; this includes assessment processes, therapeutic interventions, views of parents and children, working with groups that may be more difficult to engage such as fathers or ethnic minority groups

> papers that considered or discussed the process of decision-making within the child protection process.

Search strategy

Due to the timescales involved, four bibliographic databases were examined: ASSIA, MEDLINE, PsycINFO and CSA Social Studies Abstracts. Only studies published in peer reviewed journals were reviewed and studies eligible for inclusion included:

> those that explored the child protection process from the perspective of social workers

> those that explored the child protection process from the perspective of social work managers

> those that explored different ways of working within children's services and across multiagency teams of networks

> those that explored different assessment approaches

> those that explored different interventions

> those that explored the decision-making processes of those working within child protection.

Studies that were excluded included those that were specific interventions designed to address specific issues and from one particular perspective; for example, this could be interventions designed to address mental health or substance misuse issues from a health or youth offending perspective. Also excluded were book reviews and commentaries.

Results

The database search initially identified 8,508 articles, which reduced to 6,546 once duplicates were electronically deleted. From this around 120 abstracts were extracted from the database search for further analysis.

Appendix B

Self-assessment tool for Children's Trust Boards

A self-assessment tool that Children's Trust Boards can use to assess their governance and accountability arrangements, as well as the way they manage resources, is available through the Improvement Network:
www.improvementnetwork.gov.uk/imp/aio/1080376

The key question areas in the self-assessment tool for Children's Trust Boards to consider are:

> How far does the Children's Trust focus on improving outcomes for local children and young people?

> How does the board oversee the effective use of resources?

> What are the roles of the Children's Trust partners in delivering improvement?

> How does the board effectively consult, engage with and involve key stakeholders?

> How does the board support local capacity building and capability development?

> How are good governance and the principles of public life demonstrated by the board?

> How does the board manage risks and exercise proper controls?

Index

About the author

Jane Barlow

Jane Barlow D.Phil. FFPH (Hon) is a Professor of Public Health in the Early Years at the University of Warwick

Professor Barlow's main research interest is the role of early parenting in the aetiology of mental health problems, and in particular the evaluation of early interventions aimed at improving parenting practices, particularly during pregnancy and the postnatal period. Her programme of research focuses on interventions that are provided around infancy, and she has recently provided the evidence-base for the revised Child Health Promotion Programme (0 - 3 years). She is Director of Warwick Infant and Family Wellbeing Unit, which provides training and research in innovative evidence-based methods of supporting parenting during pregnancy and the early years. It serves a wide range of early years and primary care practitioners. She has also undertaken extensive research on the effectiveness of interventions in the field of child protection, and has produced numerous Cochrane reviews on this topic and was an author of one of the recent Lancet international reviews of what works. She recently co-authored a book on safeguarding children from emotional abuse.

Jane Scott

During 20 years of research and development projects in the field of child welfare, Jane Scott has project managed many complex studies funded by local and national government. Previous roles included Research Fellow at the Centre for Child and Family Research, University of Loughborough, and Lecturer at Dundee University.
Jane Scott currently works freelance on several research and development projects; this includes helping to set up a new service in Scotland - the Multi-Agency Resource Service (MARS) - to support practitioners and managers from all organisations working with vulnerable children and families in order to co-ordinate and broker knowledge transfer on local and national platforms, facilitate mentoring and consultancy, and provide advice.

Did this tell you what you need to know?

We want our research reviews to be useful. Both directly, in informing policy and practice, and conceptually, in providing relevant frameworks for thinking through the issues addressed.

What we do

> We consult with our Partnership network in deciding on the topic and focus for our reviews

> We work with leading academics to search research literature and policy to produce a review showing the latest evidence around each topic

> We disseminate hard copies to the **research in practice** network through our Link Officers

> We make electronic copies available on our website

What you can do

We want to know more about what happens next...

> Please take a moment to answer the two questions on the cards opposite

> Please include your email address and send the freepost card to us

We can then get in touch with you to find out how you made use of the review, and what we could do to make the next research review even better

Thank you!